SUSTAINING ACTIVISM

SUSTAINING ACTIVISM

A Brazilian
Women's Movement
and a Father-Daughter
Collaboration

JEFFREY W. RUBIN AND EMMA SOKOLOFF-RUBIN

Duke University Press
Durham and London
2013

© 2013 DUKE UNIVERSITY PRESS
All rights reserved

Printed in the United States of America on acid-free paper ∞
Designed by C. H. Westmoreland
Typeset in Arno Pro with Mido display by Keystone Typesetting, Inc.
Library of Congress Cataloging-in-Publication Data appear
on the last printed page of this book.
Title page photograph by Ellen Augarten.

To Shoshana, Hannah, and Esther, with all our love

CONTENTS

EMMA'S PREFACE

Gessi Bonês defied her father and started a women's movement when she was seventeen years old. It was 1986, and rural women in southern Brazil didn't have the right to maternity leave, pensions, or autonomy in their own homes. By 2004, Gessi's movement had transformed the lives of women across the region, successfully challenging laws that had once seemed unchangeable, and Gessi had moved from street protests to city hall. That July, my dad and I traveled together to Ibiraiaras, where Gessi and her family lived.

I was fifteen, Dad was forty-nine, and we had set out to research this women's movement as a team. During movement meetings in church basements and interviews in women's homes, we learned what was, and still is, at stake as they try to change the world. As we returned to Ibiraiaras over the next nine years, we learned that doing research abroad changes who you are at home.

When members of the Brazilian women's movement fight for legal rights and a space to speak in rural homes, they challenge deeply entrenched dynamics of gender and power. Dad and I also face conventions—who learns from whom, how fathers and daughters interact—and we try to break them through our collaboration. As the women we met in Brazil let us into their lives, and we kept returning with our writing for them to revise and share, all of us worked to forge relationships of equality across lines of power and tradition.

Ever since Dad and I returned from our first research trip in 2004, friends have asked us what it meant for women who as teenagers defied their fathers to start a movement to see me doing research with my father at just that age. I don't know for sure, but the question has made me wonder about comments that didn't seem significant at the time. What was Gessi's sister, Ivone Bonês, signaling when she said that her father never listened to her? Why did Gessi always introduce us as "Jeffrey and his daughter Emma"? And what could we learn from Dad's graduate student, who said that watching our collaboration made her think of her own father?

Gessi, Ivone, and the other women I met in Brazil showed me the ability of ordinary people to change their communities and what it takes to keep protesting, speaking, and envisioning new ways to reform the world. I learned from their dedication, but not only from their success. Maybe because I was a teenager when we met, maybe because Dad and I came as a team, they let us into the hard parts of activism: the moments when silence stifles conversation, the difficulty of staying committed to a vision of the world different from that in which you live, and the ongoing question of where and how to fight for change.

When I brought my daughter to southern Brazil to study a women's movement, I knew we were stepping into the middle of a grand arc of social change. Across the vast country, ordinary Brazilians waged a grassroots battle against hunger, poverty, and violence. In the 1980s, they pressed a military dictatorship to accept democracy. In 2002, a nation that had become a laboratory for democracy elected a progressive union leader to the presidency. And in 2010, Brazilians chose Dilma Rousseff, a woman and former leftist guerrilla, as president.

From the beginning of this transformation, the activists in the rural women's movement brought issues of gender equality and women's rights into public spaces. In their *luta* (struggle), they fought for two kinds of rights simultaneously—big economic changes that needed to come from state legislatures and the national government in Brasilia, and daily freedoms that could be won only in local communities and at home.

As we did research together, Emma and I came to understand that this battle went beyond standing up to the police or facing multinational corporations head-on. Hearing rural women's stories, we saw how fighting to change the world and to live your life differently is fraught on the inside with conflict and loneliness, nostalgia and shame. We did not know going in how much it cost individual women—and a women's movement—to put into words the exclusions they suffered and make them into public demands.

We also never imagined how much our relationship as father and daughter would change as we saw firsthand the private pains and triumphs behind Brazil's political transformation. As we grappled to understand the women's enchantment with activism, Emma and I moved from being parent and child, writing in one improvised voice, to working as colleagues, writing in our own alternating voices chapter by chapter.

The women's movement takes shape in big demonstrations, where lines of farmwomen march forward in the face of armed police. It deepens in movement-run pharmacies in the back rooms of houses and union halls, where thick syrups and sweet-scented salves make space for conversation and healing. The political way forward is rarely clear, and re-forming gender roles is so difficult that after years of struggle, you have to look hard to identify what you've achieved, though you know it's there.

In getting to these places, my unexpected research partner was my daughter. As we work to hammer out new forms of scholarship, and to understand our own world better, we are drawn in by the activism that keeps Brazilian women running for office and mobilizing in the streets for rights. In a world of silencing and violence, their bid to re-enchant democracy is a gamble we want to bet on.

Map of Rio Grande do Sul, Brazil. *Map by Bill Nelson.*

PART I

Origins

1

LEAVING HOME

Emma

Gessi Bonês and Vera Fracasso were teenagers when they founded a women's movement that would transform the lives of women in southern Brazil. Two decades later, the movement—and the stories of the women who dared to start something their friends and family believed would fail—had a powerful impact on me. When Gessi and Vera talk about the early days of the movement, their stories sometimes have the sound of distant reflections. But when they try to explain what so enchanted them about activism, and how their lives and the movement they created have changed, they speak with the mix of passion and uncertainty they felt when they were my age.

Vera's father made all the decisions at home during her childhood. Her parents worked side by side in the fields, struggling to make a living on their small family farm. Her father made decisions about what crops to plant, when to harvest them, and what products to sell at markets in nearby towns. Her mother worked on the farm, prepared meals, cleaned the house, and washed laundry by hand. "She participated in the work," Vera told me in one of our earliest conversations, "but never expressed opinions or made decisions." When Vera asked her mother why she hardly spoke at home, her mother responded that life had always been that way.

Vera wasn't content with her mother's silence. "I never accepted that," Vera said, but daily realities resisted her at every turn: like most young women who grew up in the southern Brazilian countryside in the 1980s, Vera had to ask permission to leave the house. The difficulty of daily farmwork, paired with long-standing beliefs about men's and women's roles in the household, meant that there was little space in rural homes for conversation. Good soil and plentiful water allowed many rural families in Vera's state, Rio Grande do Sul, to achieve basic economic security, but solid wooden houses and a modest cash crop did not bring schooling beyond primary grades, access to basic medical care, or an escape from the authority of fathers accustomed to being in control. Even as the physical touchstones of modernity became available to rural Brazilians in the mid-1980s, new agricultural policies made it even more difficult for family farms to compete with large landowners and agricultural corporations.[1] Vera watched her father work to end corruption in the local farmers' union and admired his commitment to making the union a reliable

Gessi Bonês. *Photographer unknown.*

force for defending farmers, but the only workers the union took seriously were men.

Gessi's father also worked in the unions. He had "a vision of participation," she remembers, "and of fighting for rights for farmers." Gessi learned about political organizing from her father and about a different kind of organizing from her mother, who worked on the farm and managed to divide food, farmwork, and household chores among her nine children. Gessi didn't start school until she was nine—it was too much of a burden to get there every day—and when she did start, she walked five kilometers each way, missing two of the next six school years due to sickness. In the winter, she left for school before the sun rose. "We didn't have the road you drove here on," she told me two decades later, "so I walked through forest, on rocks." Growing up, Gessi saw up close the difficulty of everyday life and didn't believe things had to be that way.

Local priests and nuns were the first to take seriously Gessi and Vera's refusal to accept the limitations of their parents' way of life. Bishop Orlando Dotti of Rio Grande do Sul was known for his commitment to liberation theology, a radical current that had been gaining ground within the Catholic Church. Along with other leaders in the liberation theology movement of his time, Bishop Orlando insisted on incorporating the fight for social change into his religious practices and was committed to using his power as representative of the Church to initiate and strengthen this fight.[2]

In the 1960s, when teenagers in the United States were taking to the streets and beginning to speak about citizenship and sexuality in new ways, Brazil was seized by a military dictatorship that would rule through violent repression for the next twenty years. Citizens who dared to continue protests in the 1970s risked and often lost their lives.[3] So the 1980s, the decade when Brazilians overthrew the military dictatorship and could discuss politics and protest against the government without as high a risk of arrest, was in many ways Brazil's version of the 1960s: a moment of possibility and determination that stood in stark contrast to the past. But for Brazilian teenagers in the 1980s, the past was darker than it had been for their American counterparts two decades earlier. Gessi and Vera didn't experience police brutality firsthand until they joined social movements in the mid-1980s, but they still experienced the 1985 transition to democracy against a backdrop of torture and death. Like many Brazilians of their generation, they were both cautious and desperate for change.

For supporters of liberation theology in Brazil's Catholic Church (liberationists), the political shifts of the 1980s led to a period of rapid internal change.

Conditions in rural Brazil improved after the military dictatorship ended, but liberationist nuns and priests, who worked closely with community members and communicated with a wider network of clergy across the country, saw that poverty and violence endured. They developed new ways of thinking about Jesus, the Bible, and the Church itself, and they approached their work with an unprecedented level of commitment to improving the material conditions of poor Brazilians and to helping people live with voice and dignity.

The priests and nuns organized youth groups in which rural teenagers discussed issues of gender and inequality, grappling in new ways with the challenges they faced as a nation and in their daily lives. Father Cláudio Prescendo, a priest in the small town of Sananduva, where Gessi grew up, observed "the harm of concentrated wealth, of large landholdings, of neo-liberalism and free-trade agreements that benefit the richest groups," and he thought youths would be the most powerful force in countering these harms. Father Cláudio brought busloads of rural teens to nearby shantytowns, just as other clergy had brought him to work in poverty-stricken areas as a teenager. Though many rural families worried about income and food on a daily basis, most of them had shelter and land. This exposure to a different reality, guided by nuns and priests, was instrumental in providing a broader sense of Brazil to teenagers who, according to Father Cláudio, "had never left their worlds." Many of the people who went on to lead social movements trace their activism to these youth groups, which changed their understanding of the world and of their power as citizens.

Did parents want their children to change? Gessi's parents were less concerned about what she learned at the meetings than about her going alone. They didn't mind when she went with her brother, but when he was out on a date or with friends, they always tried to keep her from going to the meetings. Even when Gessi's older sister Ivone began to participate, their parents resisted letting the two sisters travel alone. The social conventions they were fighting against—the silencing of women, the control of fathers over their daughters' lives—often kept Gessi and Ivone at home.

That's not to say the guys had a free ride. Gessi's husband, Ari Benedetti (known as Didi), also faced resistance from his family. When I asked Didi's father how his son and daughter-in-law got involved in activism, he threw up his hands and laughed, "When the priests came!" Didi's father wasn't always so easygoing. When Didi asked to join the church youth group as a teenager, his father said no. Father Cláudio worked hard to convince Didi's parents to let their son participate, returning for three consecutive dinners in a marathon effort to win them over. At other teens' houses, priests or nuns played cards, stayed for dinner, and, if parents still hadn't changed their minds, came back the next week. While the priests lived nearby, many of the nuns traveled from other towns and spent the night with the teenagers' families.

The Church formed a central part of community life in Sananduva, a regional commercial center of fourteen thousand people whose busy main street was surrounded by blocks of brightly colored houses and long stretches of farmland. Priests and nuns carried out baptisms and funerals, and they were the public figures to whom people turned in moments of sickness and economic uncertainty. Aside from wooden farmhouses, which rarely had more than a few rooms, local churches were the only spaces in which community gatherings could take place. Clergy in Sananduva and surrounding towns gained authority from their religious position, but that position did not dictate distance from the community the way it might have elsewhere. For Didi's mother, who attended mass every Sunday, going to church was an excuse to leave her house, and she grew close to the neighbors and religious leaders she met there. Didi's father told his wife that if anything happened to Didi, she would be to blame for trusting the priests. But he didn't stop his son from joining the church youth group. Didi told me this in his parents' house, looking out at the fields where he worked when he was a teenager and walked the unpredictable line between what his father tolerated and what he refused to accept. Didi ran home from the fields each evening, stopped to shower, then sprinted six kilometers to the church for youth group meetings, his dark, curly hair damp with water and sweat. "Sometimes I got a ride back home," he told me, "and sometimes I walked."

Part of the draw of the youth groups for Gessi, Ivone, Vera, and Didi was the possibility of thinking about the world in a different way, of envisioning a future that was different from the world in which they lived. Equally enticing was the chance to take a break from the fields, leave the house, and escape the isolation of life on rural farms. When the government announced plans to construct dams that would flood parts of Sananduva and other towns, priests helped local teenagers form an antidam movement by making T-shirts and posters and organizing demonstrations in the streets. "There are two types of societies," Gessi believed then and believes now: "The more equal society is the one in which people participate, in which people have a right to work, home, food, and education. And the other is the society in which we live . . .

and we need to participate, organize, mobilize to say we don't agree with this society." While Gessi's first experience with activism was shaped by this long-term goal, the urgency behind her work came from the immediate need of small towns and small farmers to survive.

In 1985, in the midst of the nascent antidam movement, Gessi left Sananduva for a convent in Passo Fundo, a city eighty-eight kilometers from Sananduva and about ten times the size. The most progressive thinkers and activists she knew were priests and nuns, and she wanted to be like them. She was sixteen, knew she wanted to work for social change, and figured the best way to improve the lives of rural families was to become a nun.

That idea didn't last long. Gessi arrived at the convent in February and by April had already butted heads with the nuns. Instead of studying biblical passages with an eye toward fighting injustice and inequality, as she had in the youth groups, at the convent Gessi learned only the most literal approaches to religious texts. She observed with increasing frustration that the nuns there didn't share her commitment to changing the world. The nuns spoke about building community, but they always ate at a separate table from the girls and assigned the most difficult chores to Gessi and the two other girls who had grown up on farms. The nuns talked in vague terms about helping the poor, but, in Gessi's eyes, they wanted to have nothing to do with ordinary people.

While at the convent, Gessi studied religion with the nuns and attended night courses at a local school to complete fifth grade. At the school, she saw the violent and drug-ridden realities of urban life more intensely than she had on trips with Father Cláudio. In May, several of her night school teachers went on strike, and Gessi immediately spoke up in their defense. The nuns were not pleased. The strike gained momentum, classes stopped temporarily, and Gessi went home, intending to stay and work on the antidam movement. Her father, from whom she inherited her firm will, told her, "You wanted to go, you're going to finish the year."

In the end, Gessi is glad she returned to the convent, though the nuns' strict rules and narrow worldview drove her crazy. "In the convent I learned to defend what I believe," she said. Perched on a staircase cleaning walls at the end of the year, Gessi told one of the nuns, Noeli de Mello, what she thought of the convent. "This convent is going to shut down," she said. "It's going to end with you, because you say one thing and do another." Sister Noeli waited until the walls were clean and then reported the incident to the head nun, who approached Gessi and invited her out for ice cream. "I said no," Gessi told me, face flushed as it must have been then: "I wouldn't be bought." She had already made her decision: "the convent wasn't where I would be able to work to change people's lives." This was the first time Gessi struggled to find a place where she could be the kind of political activist she thought necessary to change the world.

When Gessi finished her time at the convent and returned to the youth group run by Father Cláudio, similar groups were flourishing throughout the state. With the priests' support, representatives from each group met in Passo Fundo. The teenagers discussed the antidam campaign and ways of pressuring national leaders to use government funds to feed Brazilians rather than pay off external debt. They opted to participate in the unions and in politics, and a group of young women decided that they should organize around women's issues, though they didn't yet know how. "The image of youth was of kids, drugs, and music," Gessi said, "and we were trying to show that rural teenagers had value and knew how to do things, how to produce and how to organize."

For many teenagers, this meeting was the first time they visited Passo Fundo. Gessi remembers thinking that going there was like going to "the end of the world"—an unimaginably distant place. Didi remembers his first trip to Porto Alegre, a city of 1.2 million six hours away by bus, with a mix of awe and nervousness that hasn't abated with the years. "I arrived there and looked out the window," he said, describing his arrival in Porto Alegre two decades ago. "How could a place be so big? I didn't even know how to ask directions to the place I was going. I was so scared, I bought another ticket and went back home." Father Cláudio remembers that when he first visited rural homes to persuade parents to let their children join the youth groups, the teenagers, including Gessi and Didi, were quiet and shy. They had never planned demonstrations, traveled to cities, or spoken in public alone.

Gessi had no intention of speaking out loud when she and Valesca Orsi, a nun in her twenties, stood before a group of priests and asked for their support in a new project. Gessi and other young women in Sananduva had decided that the first step in organizing for women's rights would be to bring together women from different towns. They looked to the Church, which had been their entry point into politics, to help them bring in others as well. When they arrived to meet with the priests, Gessi turned to Sister Valesca and said, "you speak."

"You speak," Valesca responded. Father Cláudio opened the meeting and said, "Speak, Gessi." So Gessi stood and made her case, deftly describing the project and telling the priests she was counting on them to encourage women in their parishes to join discussions about women's rights. "Continue on with that diplomacy," Bishop Orlando said as Gessi sat down. As she left the room, Gessi turned to Valesca and asked, "What's diplomacy?"

Rural teens gained confidence and skill through their work with liberationist priests. But when Gessi and her peers put into practice the ability to speak, to organize, and to imagine and strive for new horizons, they found that the priests were willing to go only so far, and that the lines they drew were unpredictable. Though the priests encouraged demonstrations against the government, some refused to stand behind the teenagers' decision to challenge corruption in the local union by running an opposition slate in upcoming elections. Gessi still doesn't know why priests withdrew support at that moment. One reason may have been that the unions were run by community members rather than distant government officials, and the conflict was getting too close to home. Another is that the priests supported the idea of accountability within the unions but opposed a grassroots, rough-and-tumble electoral campaign as a means to promote it.

The union reform campaign was the first of several conflicts with the Catholic Church. After Gessi and her friends followed through with the campaign, the priests refused to let them use a room in the local church for a meeting. Rather than cancel the meeting, she and her friends met on the front steps of the church. (Years later, after founding a movement of their own, Gessi and Ivone would spend the night on the floor of a government building when the governor refused to meet with them.) "Church leaders can be a very powerful force" in supporting social movements, Gessi explained. "But often when the people's organizations are the strongest, the Church arrives and says, 'I'll go this far, but I won't go forward.'"

The young activists went forward full force. Many became leaders in the social movements taking shape across the state: the union-reform movement, the antidam movement, and the landless workers movement. Activism became their lives. Some young men and women, including Gessi, Vera, Ivone, and Didi, left home and traveled from town to town, running meetings and organizing demonstrations in major cities. They led hundreds of small farmers on overnight bus rides, cooking meals on the side of the highway and then taking over buildings until government officials listened to their demands.

For many activists, joining social movements meant defying their parents. Didi's father tolerated his participation in church youth groups, but when

Didi began to participate fully in social movements, his father gave him two options: "He told me I could do whatever I wanted, but if I was going to join the movements, I couldn't stay in his house." Didi packed his bags.

It was a moment of innovative and often dangerous protests. Landless farmers across the state had begun taking over large plots of idle farmland, entire families facing down policemen, soldiers, and private paramilitaries. Often women and children stood at the front lines when the military arrived, and liberationist priests joined the protests in an effort to curb the violence, which nonetheless took activists' lives. Land takeovers were bold, risky, and effective, and within ten years the Landless Workers' Movement, known as the MST (Movimento dos Trabalhadores Rurais Sem Terra), became the largest social movement in Brazil.

Unequal land distribution was, and still is, one of the foremost contributors to poverty in Brazil. In the 1970s, fearing that discontent across the countryside might lead to revolt, leaders of the military dictatorship took steps to make land reform legal. As Brazil moved toward democracy in the 1980s, politicians and activists across the political spectrum expected that significant land reform would be part of the transition from dictatorship to democracy. However, wealthy landowners, who controlled politics in rural areas and had the largest voting bloc in the national congress, organized legally and extra-legally to protect their property. Instead of actually mandating land redistribution, the new constitution developed under democracy created a framework for land reform, but included no requirement that it be carried out.

Didi and Gessi didn't need land for themselves, but people they knew did, and land distribution was part of the societal change they wanted to create. Along with other young activists who supported the MST, they spent nights camped on large plots of idle land, sleeping in tents made of canvas or sheets of black plastic. They joined activists who lived full time on the *acampamentos* (encampments), refusing to leave until the government agreed to seize the land from wealthy landowners and give it to landless farmers—or until judges ordered the activists to move or landowners hired their own paramilitaries to force protesters off the land. Squatters responded by establishing new encampments on other idle land, at prominent crossroads, or along the sides of highways, living in the makeshift tents for months and often years in order to pressure the government to expropriate the land they claimed as theirs.

In 2004, the summer I turned fifteen, Gessi opened a scrapbook on her kitchen table to show me some of the moments I had missed. In photographs of protests and confrontations with armed policemen, she is only two years older than me. Her shoulder-length auburn hair shines red in the sunlight. A head shorter than most of the male leaders, face a blur of emotions and ideas, she appears caught in motion: raising her arms to wave a Brazilian flag, conferring with other leaders, or ripping through a crowd of activists and tear gas. "Do you know what a bayonet looks like?" she asked, and then, without waiting for my answer, turned the page to show six parked and loaded buses facing a line of policemen with bayonets and dogs across an open field. Peaceful demonstrations were often met with violence, and many of her friends got hurt. At one demonstration, she told me, the police outnumbered the activists three to one. "But then we started moving," Gessi remembered, "and the dogs and policemen started to walk backward, walk backward, and we kept walking forward. The police went back and we walked forward, holding hands and flags, singing, singing, singing. But the police could have reacted differently, could have attacked us with dogs or tear gas. Those are moments of a lot of responsibility."

Moments of responsibility were also moments of uncertainty. When the police arrived and Gessi told the people she had persuaded to leave their homes, travel to a city they'd never visited, and protest against the government that they should walk forward, she didn't know if the police would retreat or attack. If she had made the wrong decision, she and her friends could have been killed. And even if no one died, a mistaken calculation or an overly daring decision would have jeopardized the cause for which she had asked people to put their lives on the line.

In moments like these, Gessi had no protocol to guide her decisions. What she had were other leaders, who were also young, passionate, dedicated, and unsure.

Didi entered the kitchen and looked over Gessi's and my shoulders at the photographs. In one image, he stands with his fist in the air and his mouth open in song. Didi didn't think of himself as a leader until he stood at the front of demonstrations, searching for the right words when it mattered most. He remembers grabbing the microphone in moments like the one I saw on the scrapbook page, not knowing what to say but knowing the tremendous responsibility that came with holding the microphone in his hand.

At twenty years old, Vera was a leader of the union-reform movement her father had once refused to let her join. Despite her small frame, she learned to command attention with her sharp facial features and strong words. She spent her days running protests in the streets and meeting with leaders to plan the next campaign. But her efforts to reform unions and secure government support for small farmers wasn't changing what had first drawn her to activism: the silencing of women on rural farms and the legal and social inequalities that she faced each day. Vera cared about dams and debt and unions. But she also cared about being able to leave the house without asking permission, and about the possibility of a marriage in which she wouldn't be the only one responsible for housework and childcare. Vera didn't want the life her mother lived. She wanted to have a say in economic decisions and a voice in conversations at the dinner table.

Vera and Gessi knew that when their mothers retired from daily work in the fields, they would receive no pensions and would be economically dependent on their husbands. The two young women had already begun to imagine lives that weren't based entirely on the farm. But they wanted rural women of their mothers' generation and of their own to have the right to pensions and maternity leave, and the official documentation that would entitle them to legal rights.

The male leaders with whom Gessi and Vera worked weren't interested in incorporating women's issues into social-movement campaigns. In the men's eyes, land, debt, and dams came first, and only after addressing poverty and hunger would there be time to fight for women's rights. When the young women persisted, male leaders told them to form women's groups in existing movements—essentially saying, you can talk about these issues on your own, so long as you stay committed to what this movement is really about.

Gessi and Vera didn't think a movement had to be about only one thing. They were spending almost every day helping run social movements, and they wanted those movements to recognize women's rights as a central concern. When male leaders continued to push aside this issue—and the women who brought it to the table—Gessi, Vera, and other young women leaders began to envision their own movement. Their movement would take on issues of class and gender simultaneously. It wouldn't ignore the threat of large agricultural corporations, or the need for union reform, but it wouldn't pretend that these were the only issues at stake in rural women's lives. To young women who had grown up on farms, issues of silence, isolation, and legal rights weren't secondary—they were central to the fabric of everyday life.

The young women still wondered if an autonomous movement was necessary. They didn't want to weaken existing movements by forming their own. Loiva Rubenich, for example, joined the MST because she believed in agrarian reform, and because she and her husband needed land. She had been forced to quit school after ninth grade to care for her brothers, who continued studying, and she wanted the men in her life to take seriously her needs and ideas. But Loiva didn't want to give up fighting for land, and she didn't want to leave the MST. So when other MST leaders insisted that land came first and women's rights would follow, Loiva listened.

She soon found that when a movement fought for land first and women second, women got left behind. As leaders, they were often pushed aside, sent to look after children while the male leaders planned protests. When women did participate, Loiva said, it felt like their ideas "were never heard." Loiva remembers reminding her colleagues at a protest-planning meeting that women and children would also be present at the protest and needed to be factored into the plan. She was almost kicked out of the meeting.

Loiva hoped that once she and her husband secured a piece of land, she could focus on fighting for women's rights, and the two of them could find ways to create equality in their relationship. But once they had land, her husband, who had supported her participation in the struggle for agrarian reform, wanted her to stay home. "What happened was that once the families were settled," Loiva explained, "they went back to the system in which they used to live: the woman inside the house and the man taking over the public spaces. For me, that was a very difficult situation. I had a son, I was married, and for me this didn't mean I would stay inside the four walls of my house. My way of living wasn't accepted, my way of leaving, working, participating in politics. I was reminded many times that my work was to stay home and take care of my son."

Loiva, Gessi, and Vera refused to stay home. Instead, they founded a women's movement.

When Gessi, Vera, and Loiva first told me about the early days of the movement, it sounded almost seamless: they decided that women's issues should take center stage, tore through the resistance of their fathers and male colleagues, and started a new movement. But as our conversations continued, I realized that the reality was much less straightforward. Women's movements had already taken shape in urban centers in Brazil, but rural women had little contact with feminist organizers in cities and no model on which to base a women's movement. Father Cláudio and Bishop Orlando supported the young women's decision to form an autonomous women's movement—a surprise, after the Catholic Church's mixed response to the local union-reform campaign—but the young women still faced the challenge of mobilizing rural women who had to ask their husbands' or fathers' permission to leave the house.

Male leaders of existing social movements weren't about to help. "Now these farmwomen are going to want to talk about participating in organizations, participating in social life, in the economy and everything!" Vera remembers hearing variations of this argument again and again. The men were right: Vera did mean for the movement to change society in fundamental ways, and push both women and men to "value things they hadn't valued before."

Gessi and Vera had learned to seize the microphone in crucial moments of protest and speak with confidence and strength. But they had never started a movement, and standing up to policemen was easier than defying their families and many of their friends. When Gessi, Vera, and other women speak about this part of their lives, I wonder if they wondered if the women's movement—this daring idea, this vision of change—would work at all.

TRANSFORMING SOUTHERN BRAZIL
Jeff

Fighting for reform in Brazil means challenging harsh realities. Brazil has been a democracy since 1985 and boasts the sixth-largest economy in the world, but these achievements have not translated into inclusion or decent standards of living for vast numbers of Brazilians. Brazil's inequality has a long history. In the nineteenth century, Brazil was the largest slaveholding society in the Western Hemisphere, the last country to end slavery, and the hemisphere's only monarchy. When slavery was abolished in 1888, the country's landowners and urban elites did not consider the freed slaves fit for wage labor or incorporation into society. So they subsidized the immigration to Brazil of hundreds of thousands of poor Italians and other Europeans, many of whom settled in Rio Grande do Sul, to do the backbreaking work of plantation agriculture, colonize land for small farms, and, later on, man the factories of a growing industrial economy, alongside the descendants of slaves.[1]

In the 1930s, President Getulio Vargas managed the dual demands of industrialization and mass participation by establishing a dictatorship that accorded some significant cultural inclusion and economic benefits. Vargas's Estado Novo (New State) recast and celebrated Brazil as a mixed-race nation (though in reality this brought few gains to the still marginalized black population) and incorporated urban workers into a national system of labor unions that granted the workers economic benefits while strictly controlling their union activities and political choices. In the countryside there was no such exchange. Large landowners and rural political bosses, intertwined in powerful networks of elite families, ruled through a politics of clientelism and favors and an economy of mass poverty.[2]

Today Brazil is one of the most unequal countries in the world. The shantytowns of ultramodern cities like São Paulo and Rio de Janeiro have come to symbolize the desperate and enduring poverty of Latin America, which recent democratic governments have been struggling, with limited success, to ameliorate.[3] Brazil is an agricultural powerhouse—among the largest exporters of soy, oranges, coffee, sugar, and beef in the world—but many of the women we met grew and prepared their own food and had to struggle to send their

Regional movements block the highway. *Photo by Arquimedes Sassi; used with permission.*

children to the doctor and pay basic school fees. Southern Brazil is heavily populated by the descendants of poor European immigrants, so the stereotypes of poor Brazilians as dark skinned are belied by the fair complexions of people there. Many of them face poverty, unemployment, and, for those with small landholdings, the danger of losing their land. In a country where the rule of law is uneven at best, those who fight for change in the countryside face police hostility and paramilitary violence.

The crisis that now threatens small farmers in Rio Grande do Sul began with the rural development policies of Brazil's military dictatorship. The tool that farmers have used to fight back, the rural unions, dates to the same period.[4] In the 1970s, surveying an unproductive countryside and a Western Hemisphere marked by rural rebellions and guerrilla warfare from Mexico to Argentina, Brazil's military decided to promote large-scale corporate agriculture and finally incorporate rural workers, including small farmers, into the union structure. New agricultural policies offered landowners in Rio Grande do Sul credit and cheap inputs for large-scale production of wheat and soy, rather than for the more diversified set of products that had long been the mainstay of farming in the state and included the foods people consumed at home, such as corn and cassava. The union component of the military's rural-development program provided men who worked in the countryside with limited but significant economic benefits, such as small pensions and some access to health care, through a national union that remained closely controlled by the government.

The development model pursued by the military, based on mechanized production on vast tracts of land, laid the groundwork for the agricultural expansion that has driven Brazil's economic growth in the 2000s and 2010s. The model also threatened the livelihoods of small farmers, who still hold approximately 43 percent of the land in the state of Rio Grande do Sul and account for 57 percent of its agricultural production.[5] These small farmers became dependent on credit to buy seeds, fertilizer, and machinery. They produced less and less of the food they and their neighbors consumed, and they saw land around them bought up by large landowners and corporations. The children of many small farmers left the countryside, often for a life of poverty in urban shantytowns, which expanded exponentially during this period. Many of the farmers, however, along with increasing numbers of their children, learned to make use of the union structure to fight back. With the backing of priests and nuns schooled in liberation theology, they fielded progressive slates in union elections and gradually, in the course of the 1980s and after, won key positions in towns across the state. Local battles—for credit, health care, land, and new approaches to agriculture—started with the unions and continued in them, because it was through the unions that farmers secured the legal identity of "rural workers" and gained access to social security.

As military dictatorship gave way to elections and then to the process of writing a new Brazilian constitution, the young people who began their activism in the unions went beyond where their fathers were willing to go. Faced with vast inequality in landholdings and plans to destroy whole communities by constructing a network of dams that would advance even further the agenda of large-scale modernization, the young activists formed new, more radical movements.[6] It was in these movements that the views of young women like Gessi and Vera, who refused to accept the limits their mothers faced, fused with the broader historical moment. If they could win the legal designation of "rural worker," women who toiled long hours alongside their husbands on family farms would gain access to pensions in their own names and paid maternity leave. And if they participated in unions and became leaders, they could play a role in shaping rural-development policies, finding economic alternatives for small farmers, improving inadequate health-care services, and breaking the isolation and silence that characterized the lives of women on family farms.[7]

Church youth groups taught the young women they could turn these ideas into action. The Catholic Church in Rio Grande do Sul had established seminaries for men and then women early in the twentieth century, and the immigrant families who settled there encouraged their children to pursue religious vocations. By the 1950s, prominent Brazilian theologians turned their attention to the poverty of the countryside and the need to promote education, strengthen families, and train small farmers to navigate the agricultural modernization that was under way. The nuns and priests who adopted liberation theology in Rio Grande do Sul in subsequent decades had grown up in the region, giving them an identity rooted in local communities. They were thus in a unique position to understand the personal as political, as well as religious, and they taught their parishioners that politics was to be found in the ways they lived their daily lives, not just in electoral campaigns and government offices.

Nuns in the rural communities of Rio Grande do Sul pressed women to insist on rights and participation in the unions. The nuns went from house to house, often with young women activists like Vera and Gessi by their sides, telling women that they had rights and encouraging them to come to meetings to secure them. The nuns had themselves lived the exclusion faced by girls and women on family farms, as well as the subordinate position of women within the Catholic Church. When they spoke with farmwomen, the nuns brought the authority of experience to their claims for women's rights. They also brought religious legitimation and blessing to what otherwise seemed so daring as to be impermissible—insisting on the rights and participation of women in rural society.

Because of the work of the nuns and priests, as well as the keen sense of injustice the young women themselves were feeling, the debates and union battles coursing through the countryside in the 1980s prompted many women, young and older alike, to leave their houses and make claims for themselves and their families in public places, like union halls and local chapels (*capelas*). This occurred as activists from across Brazil were organizing grassroots campaigns, attending national meetings, and joining marches on Brasília, the nation's capital, to shape the new constitution. From cities and countryside, universities and political parties, government offices and associations of lawyers and journalists, citizens in Brazil's new democracy insisted on the need to guarantee economic and political rights and to establish institutionalized processes of popular participation in government.

At the time, nobody knew if the transition from military dictatorship to democracy in 1985 would take hold or whether the new democracy would reverse Brazil's long history of inequality and exclusion. Grassroots activists felt sure that democracy wouldn't bring change if the needs and voices of poor people weren't part of the debate, loudly and clearly. The newly formed leftist political party, the Workers' Party (Partido dos Trabalhadores), melded social movements with those who wanted to go the electoral route, pursuing mobilization in the streets and political campaigning simultaneously. Coalitions of women's groups worked tirelessly to ensure that women workers be accorded the same rights as men in the constitution, and the rural unions and newly forming rural women's groups insisted that the designation "rural worker" be applied to women who labored on farms.[8]

This was how young women in the Rio Grande do Sul countryside first claimed new kinds of rights for themselves and their mothers. Lacking even the birth certificates and social-security cards that would make them officially "people," they refused to accept that as their country became democratic and the government began treating people as citizens, women should continue to be excluded from participation outside the home and decision making within. Elenice Pastore, now a university professor, describes her reaction when her father refused to allow her to stay in school past eighth grade. "I know that I cried," Elenice remembered. "I cried for two days, but okay, patience. Two years passed, and I decided that I was going to continue my studies."

"What changed?" I asked her.

"It was because I was participating in the women's movement," Elenice responded, going on to tell us about walking along the road at six in the morning so she could get to town to take a bus to a movement meeting, knowing she would face her father's anger when she got back home, and every time after that when she had to ask him for bus fare to get to a meeting. "So sometimes I went crying," Elenice said, and I pictured her as she might have looked then, blond hair pulled back and her rounded face set with determination. "I did that walk crying in the dark, the cold, the rain. 'Okay,' I told myself, 'I'm going because I want to go to that meeting, because it's important.' "

Again and again, we encountered women whose stories began with leaving the house. As a result of the conflicts this engendered, the rural women's movement was about ordinary speech as much as formal rights. When you want to go out to a meeting, how do you discuss your plan with your father or husband, rather than ask his permission? What words do you use? And after the meeting, how do you get the governor to provide credit for small farmers, and how do you live with your husband at home?

The rural women's movement of Rio Grande do Sul officially began in 1986, when politicized teenagers, activist nuns, and middle-aged farmwomen created local women's associations, collectively called Farmwomen (Mulheres da Roça), in a number of small towns in the northern region of the state, where Ibiraiaras and Sananduva are located.[9] The women in these associations then formed a statewide organization, the Movement of Rural Women Workers, known as the MMTR (Movimento de Mulheres Trabalhadoras Rurais), in 1989, soon after Brazil's new constitution recognized women involved in agriculture as "rural workers" and accorded them the same social-security pensions, maternity leaves, and health-care benefits guaranteed to male and female workers in cities. In choosing the name MMTR, the women underscored their role as rural workers, on small farms and in MST settlements, connecting

their convictions about class inequality and workers' rights to their commitment to gender equality and women's rights.[10] Linking hundreds of neighborhood groups in small towns across the state to regional and statewide networks, the rural women's movement in Rio Grande do Sul mobilized more
than five thousand women in its first decade, reaching many more through
family and friendship ties.[11] The MMTR also established close relations with
rural women's movements in Brazil's southern states of Santa Catarina, Paraná, Mato Grosso do Sul, and São Paulo, with whom they coordinated campaigns that focused on national legislation in Brasilia.

The early national campaigns of the 1980s, in the years just after the Farmwomen's associations began, focused on influencing the elected assembly in
Brasilia that was charged with producing the new constitution. The resulting
constitution did guarantee economic rights to rural women. However, it
quickly became clear to movement activists that securing these rights in
practice would take a whole other battle, one that would come to form the
core of the MMTR's organizing efforts through the first half of the 1990s and
gain it the commitment and loyalty of tens of thousands of rural women.

Constitutional rights, it turned out, required enabling legislation, which in
turn required that bureaucracies establish procedures to carry out the laws
and then actually implement them. For pensions, the process was so slow and
ineffective in its many stages that few believed rural women would ever
receive pension checks. Even worse, President Fernando Collor, who took
office a year after the constitution was adopted, vetoed the legislation on
maternity leave for rural women entirely, stopping the implementation process in its tracks and leaving the future of the newly secured right in doubt.

In response to the disconnect between what the constitution said and what
occurred on the ground, women in the MMTR in Rio Grande do Sul joined
with women in rural women's movements nationwide to bring grassroots
pressure to bear on legislators in state capitals and in Brasilia. The women
collected signatures, formed caravans that converged on the national capital
at key moments, led demonstration after demonstration, took over buildings,
and occupied the floors of state legislatures. They learned to do these new and
disruptive acts as they went along, borrowing tactics from the other social
movements and improvising new ones. To succeed, they had to convince rural
women who rarely ventured out in public to follow them and risk police
violence in doing so. The activists gained force by making use of their identities as women at key political moments: to evade detection when they entered

the state legislature in order to occupy it; to gain attention when they con-verged on Brasilia for a massive demonstration; and to persuade skeptics when the women argued that their roles in seeing rural families through agricultural crises earned them the right to have rights.

MMTR leaders also lobbied key legislators, a strategy the women honed as they campaigned to overturn the president's veto on maternity rights, and learned to do politics inside the institutions among elected officials as well as in the streets. And then, in 1994 as the almost ten-year process of gaining constitutional rights and implementing them neared completion, they saw that women could not get their pensions without the proper documentation, including birth certificates and proof that they had been involved in the production and sale of agricultural goods. Nationwide, only about 20 percent of rural women had documentation of their existence and work life, a figure that reached 30 percent in Rio Grande do Sul. In 1994, together with the network of rural women's organizations in the south of Brazil, the MMTR undertook a documentation campaign encouraging women to secure the paperwork that would prove their existence and thus their eligibility for rights. In 1995, women from seventeen states met in São Paulo to form the National Organization of Rural Women Workers, known as ANMTR (Articulação Na-cional de Mulheres Trabalhadoras Rurais), which took up and expanded the documentation project.[12]

The MMTR developed in tandem with changes in production and in the gender division of labor on family farms, so that by the 1990s, economic changes and women's political organizing reinforced one another. In order to survive in the face of declining revenues from mechanized soy production, family farmers developed new agricultural strategies that included expanding dairy production, renewing production for auto-consumption, developing new products that could be processed on the farm and commercialized lo-cally, and combining multiple sources of agricultural and even nonagricul-tural income. In many of these cases, women took on new forms of work, or else the work women had already been doing, such as milking the cows, tending family gardens, and producing cheeses and jams, became more ex-plicitly linked in their and their husbands' minds to income generation. As a result, during the same years that women were beginning to see themselves as having rights to pensions and a say in family decisions, and to organize politically for those rights, the work they were doing on family farms was no longer seen primarily as an aid to the masculine activity of mechanized, mono-crop agriculture. Rather, women's work was central to the economic sustainability of diversifying family farms.[13]

In reflecting on the *luta* (struggle) for pension rights, activists in the women's movement recount their fathers' certainty that this battle was doomed to failure, just before they tell of bringing their mothers—the very mothers who had long deferred to their own husbands' wishes and commands—to receive their first social-security checks. These checks, while small (less than US$80 a month), provided crucial resources and autonomy for women with no resources of their own. The money also made a reliable contribution to family incomes at a time when small farmers were struggling desperately to survive. Vania Zamboni's parents thought her work in the women's movement was useless until her mother received her first pension check. Vania, Ivone's partner, dragged her mother by the arm to the bank and made sure she was the very first woman in town to get her money. Ivone and Gessi's mother always encouraged them in their determination to form a women's movement, despite their father's vehement opposition. When she received her first pension money, she split it with her daughters, but didn't give her husband any.

It wasn't only the prospect of economic rights, or even gaining a voice in their own families, that drew women into the movement. It was also what they did together at meetings, which included singing and pageantry, crafts projects and self-help exercises, along with listening to lectures and discussing their experiences at home and in their communities. The nuns and the young women together developed a repertoire of ceremonies and music they called *mística*, halfway between religious rituals and folk songs, along with activities like role play, or saying your name while performing a funny gesture, or stretching a rubber band to evoke the stress you feel inside. The meetings were a destination for which women left the house and a deeply collective antidote to isolation. Meetings created a counterpublic where alternatives to the real world were put into words and enacted. Images of a different future could then be brought home, along with crafts projects and self-help strategies.[14]

Meetings also brought knowledge and discomfort, as feminist advisors from Porto Alegre came to the countryside to lead courses on women's bodies and health, beginning in 1989 and continuing through the first half of the 1990s.[15] The MMTR was always about both economics and gender. The economic part was more clear-cut, more acceptable to men, and in the end, easier to secure. Women's new economic roles corresponded to production changes on family farms, as part of the search for alternative forms of income. But women in the

MMTR say that frank discussion of women's bodies and women's roles in the household transformed their lives. In place of silence and uncertainty about matters such as menstruation and birth control, they gained information for themselves that they could also impart to their daughters. And rather than accept farm labor *and* unending housework as their fate, women could now say that men shared the food and tracked mud on the floor, so they should do dishes and sweep too. But over the course of two decades, it proved much harder to get men to share the housework than to secure economic rights through mobilizations and protests in the streets, and the new households women envisioned in the early years of the movement were painfully slow to materialize.

Achieving democracy within the women's movement proved to be a similarly uncertain process. What did it mean to be a democratic movement, and was that important? Early on, the MMTR organized itself in four tiers: small groups in tiny communities, then gradually larger groups at the municipal, regional, and state levels. In the early years of effervescent discussion and mobilization, when the Farmwomen associations were fighting to have rural women's economic rights written into the constitution and the MMTR campaigned tirelessly to turn those rights into reality, democracy seemed to mean discussion. It was embodied in the constant interaction among the movement's various levels, with ideas and suggestions for new goals and strategies transferred back and forth from local women to regional and state assemblies and leaders. Later, however, when gender equality seemed ever harder to achieve and globalization brought new political and economic threats, what it meant to make decisions democratically—regarding how to balance competing goals and how best to achieve them—was much less clear.

When social-security pensions and maternity leave were largely in place and documentation processes were under way, the MMTR launched campaigns for better credit programs for rural women and established alternative pharmacies as gathering places to counter the isolation of life on small farms and combat the illnesses that were prevalent there. In the 1990s and 2000s, the MMTR fought simultaneously for two broad goals, sustainable agriculture and women's health, in campaigns that allied the movement with national and international peasant organizations and again linked broad political struggles to the issues of daily life.

I first met Adriana Mezadri and Salete Girardi, whom Emma and I would later interview when they were leaders of the statewide MMTR, when they were attending a training course in sustainable agriculture at a program run jointly with the MST and other rural movements. Salete explained how supportive her father and brothers had been when she transformed a corner of their garden through organic farming, seeing her new knowledge as a promising path forward. Adriana, in contrast, explained that as soon as she left town to attend a new training session, her family tore down the fences she had built and destroyed her crop.

Leaders of the movement believed that to engage rural women in a project to change the world, each woman needed to see herself as a citizen with rights, and she needed a place to speak about herself. Outside the governor's office and the state and national legislatures, women waved flags and raised fists in the air. Inside their homes, they waged private and equally challenging battles, continuing to speak a language of rights and equality even when governors, policemen, and husbands refused to budge. For Vania, who grew up with six older brothers, the women's movement was the first place where her opinion mattered. Ivone said that in the space of speech and autonomy the movement created, "we felt like people."

As a result of these strategies and the commitment and tenacity behind them, women in the Brazilian countryside now have rights to maternity leaves and pensions *and* a stronger, more-respected voice within rural households. By leaving their houses and starting a movement, the activists in the women's movement changed the lives of women across Brazil. At the same time, they opened themselves up to criticism not only for speaking and acting in unconventional ways but also for bringing what had previously been private experiences into public view. And they opened themselves up to the challenge of seeing unfairness and the possibility of a different world, while living every day immersed in the harsh realities of this one.

Securing economic rights for women came to be the founding achievement of the rural women's movement, one that gained it legitimacy and won enduring loyalty from rural women of all ages. It was also a goal on which everyone, including men, could agree. Internally, what the next steps should be was less clear. In the course of their transition from daring teenagers to committed political activists, partners, and mothers, individual leaders disagreed about the strategies and goals of the MMTR. Once a tight-knit core group, facing police repression side by side and attending each other's weddings and the baptisms of their children, the activists chose different paths for pursuing women's equality. Some of them separated acrimoniously and others drifted apart, though none moved farther than a few towns away from where they had lived as teenagers. Over time, nostalgia for the unified movement of the past— and for each other—became part of the women's identities, fueling their commitment to continue making change in the present even as they face uncertainty about where and how to take their stand.

3

FAMILY TIES

Jeff

The mixture of daring public mobilization and behind-the-scenes uncertainty that I saw in Brazil is what drew me in. I wanted to know about the choices—and the tensions and setbacks—behind the public creation of citizenship that was making Brazil an enduring democracy. By the late 1990s, great poverty and inequality coexisted with innovative local and national governments and new economic successes, brought about in part by widespread grassroots activism. As a scholar interested in how social movements promote progressive change, and in whether democracies can improve people's lives, this seemed the place to be.

I applied to the MacArthur Foundation for a Research and Writing Grant to study Brazil's social movements, and I asked for enough funding to take my family with me so they would have a stake in what I was doing. My wife, Shoshana Sokoloff, worked full time as a psychiatrist in western Massachusetts, and our daughters, Emma, Hannah, and Esther, were twelve years old, six years old, and seven months old. I won the fellowship, and in 2001 we all set out for a year in the southern state of Rio Grande do Sul, where I did field research on four social movements that were transforming the Brazilian political landscape: a participatory budgeting project in the city of Porto Alegre, where we lived; the rural women's movement in Rio Grande do Sul; the MST; and the Afro Reggae Cultural Group, which teaches young children and teenagers in Rio de Janeiro's most violent and drug-ridden favelas to use music to fight racism and violence.[1]

In the course of my research, I traveled repeatedly to Ibiraiaras and Sananduva to interview MMTR leaders and attend meetings and events. The warmth of the women and loveliness of the countryside prompted me to bring my family with me on one of my trips, in March of 2002. We toured local sights, attended meetings, and ate meals in families' homes. As my wife and daughters met the leaders of the MMTR and saw them in action, and as women in the movement got to know the five of us, a connection I hadn't fully anticipated was forged. I didn't know then, however, that two years later Emma would persuade me to go back to Brazil with her, or that our collaboration as researchers would transform my relationship with my daughter and my work as a professor.

Esther Sokoloff-Rubin at an MMTR meeting. *Photograph by Jeffrey W. Rubin.*

While the activism in the women's movement grew from young women purposefully leaving their houses and their fathers to attend meetings, Emma and I left our house together to do research. Working as a team, we discerned strengths and tensions in the women's movement that we might not otherwise have noticed. We had each other to bounce ideas off of, and the women saw us grappling daily with questions of how to make decisions and balance our voices, issues familiar from their home lives and at the heart of the women's movement.

Why did Emma take the first steps in making our research trip happen? Her reasons were simultaneously straightforward and scattershot. She wanted to go back to a place that had inspired her. She loved the adventure of living in a distant place and speaking another language. She had been drawn in by the women. Emma was attending a new school with a performing arts component, and she wanted to find a place for herself in it. So we came up with the idea of doing video interviews together and making a curriculum about the MMTR. This would give our trip a purpose and provide Emma with a project when she returned. Something appealed to both of us about traveling together. The whole idea seemed like an extension of our family year in Brazil, where our home life had connected to my work in a way it didn't in the United States, and where we had seen up close the way a twenty-five-year arc of grassroots activism was pressing the limits of politics.

Did I hope, by returning to Brazil, to forge a new kind of relationship with my daughter? Or to gain deeper insight into the women's movement than I might otherwise have gained? I don't remember thinking of it that way. The trip seemed adventurous, and in a sense, we just did it. It was one of those decisions you make without really thinking about the consequences.

In 2004, a month before Emma and I were to leave, I glanced at her open closet in our downstairs hall. Knowing the struggle it took to get her to keep her clothes inside it—and the shouting matches that resulted—I wondered how we were going to survive a month together in Brazil, without the rest of our family to act as buffers. What craziness had possessed me to consider this? I had never been alone with my daughter for weeks at a time and never made decisions about her completely on my own. In fact, over the years, the roles that Shoshana and I played in our family had shifted. We were both involved in most household and parenting tasks, and we tried to balance our work lives and share the work of running a household equally. I had often been—and continue to be—one of the few men at the playground or school drop off, and I talk mostly with women to arrange playdates and dinners. However, with time the balance of who does what in running our household had shifted. I attended more to the logistics and organizing of the house, and Shoshana more to managing the lives of the girls. I did more of the discipline. She did more of the school assemblies, along with listening about friends and emotions. In short, we had taken on more conventional gender roles in parenting.

But Emma's insistence on returning to Brazil had stimulated my imagination, and we'd made plans and purchased tickets before I reconsidered. The idea of studying the women's movement and teaching about it in Emma's school seemed a good one. And traveling far had paid off many times in my life.

When Emma and I drove into Ibiraiaras—after a twenty-four-hour trip to Porto Alegre and a subsequent five-hour drive through the mountains—we didn't know where we'd be staying. I had asked Gessi, Ivone, and Vania if they could arrange something, either a house we could rent or a room in the local hotel, which I remembered as a run-down concrete building opposite the town square with a poorly lit restaurant. When we arrived at Gessi's house, where Ivone was preparing dinner, it was cold and getting dark. Ivone greeted us with her usual understated elegance, her delight apparent as we entered. Her face—quiet, thoughtful, and unobtrusive—broke into a soft smile. After a short conversation, she sent us on to the hotel to get settled, with the news that it was a new one, constructed since our last visit. But the part of town where the hotel was located was pitch-black, with trucks and construction materials all around, and the hotel was dark as well. It was only six in the evening. "This will make a great story," Emma suggested gamely. But I was really worried. Where was I bringing my daughter, I wondered, and how could I keep her safe?

It turned out that the neighborhood and the hotel were dark because of a power outage, and the glimmers of light we saw through the windows were candles set out by the owner, Perinotto, and his wife, Rosa. The hotel was indeed new, with shining glass windows and doors, a brightly polished floor, more food and attention than we could ever need, and a small, simple suite that we crafted by shifting around beds, desks, and closets in two rooms at the end of the hall.

Those rooms housed our collaboration, and from them we ventured out to meetings, campaign rallies, women's pharmacies, and kitchens. We wondered and disagreed about all sorts of things, from what questions to ask at an interview to how to manage the day. But from early on we knew that our project made sense and would work out in some way, because of the conversation between us and because of the relationships we were forming with the leaders of the women's movement and their husbands and children. We returned each evening to two laptops on two small desks, side by side. Rapidly it became apparent that Emma would type notes furiously at the end of each day, while I would write a sentence or two, stare out the window, and then get up to prepare dinner or wash dishes. For a while, I thought that I too should be writing, but soon I realized how much better Emma was at it. As I watched her take notes and talk to the women in the movement; as we talked to each other over meals, in the car, and walking down the street, gesturing with our hands and acting out interviews; as I took on the role of teacher and she the role of student; and as these roles became confounded, so that we were each learning from the other, most of my father-and-professor self-consciousness fell away, and probably some daughter self-consciousness too. It became clear that I had put myself in a new and unexpected place.

Before I ever went to Brazil, I had seen up close how political events had cultural roots and how a family member could unexpectedly change the course of research. The first time I did fieldwork in Latin America, in the 1980s, I went there with Shoshana, five years before Emma was born. We lived in the southern Mexican city of Juchitán, located in the Isthmus of Tehuantepec. This is the narrowest part of North and Central America, after Panama, between the oil deposits of the Gulf of Mexico and the shipping routes of Mexico's Pacific coast. When Shoshana and I went there, Central America was exploding in guerrilla wars and revolution, refugees were fleeing over the border from Guatemala to Mexico, and Juchitán was the site of the most radical grassroots movement in Mexico.

I've joked many times about the inhospitable environment in Juchitán. For most of the year, it is so hot there that you have to crisscross the street as you walk, just to stay in the meager shade offered by the overhangs of rooftops or the withered leaves of parched trees. In the tropical winter, winds are so fierce that you have to wipe the dust out of your eyes as you walk and the rains so torrential that mud pours into your house under the door. Finding a Zapotec-style, one-room house to live in proved impossible—nobody would rent an empty house to two foreigners—and we ended up with a modern, large, and run-down apartment in the center of town. Just walls—all bubble-gum pink— and ants streaming across them in intricate maps.

The leaders of the radical Indian movement I went to study in Juchitán, the Coalition of Workers, Peasants, and Students of the Isthmus, known as cocei (Coalición Obrera, Campesina, Estudiantil del Istmo), wouldn't talk to me for the fourteen months I lived there. As a result, I was forced to learn about politics by other means.[2] Our apartment opened onto the sprawling central market, and Shoshana and I talked to the market women as we bought household goods, fruit and vegetables, and, in the prepared foods section of the market, corn tamales and fresh cheese for breakfast. These women eventually invited us to their homes and introduced us to their families.

Thus in an intensely polarized Mexican city, where armed soldiers stood guard on the balconies of city hall twenty-four hours a day, I was welcomed in family courtyards, but not at political meetings. From this vantage point, I learned to speak Zapotec and to ask questions about daily life and radical politics. As I shared meals and attended celebrations with families committed to a leftist political movement, I learned that young girls left school to sell lemons in the market, that neighborhood protest meetings provided meeting grounds for potential spouses, and that voting offered an occasion for dressing up. The radical movement many Juchitecos joined, in turn, held divergent meanings and goals simultaneously. I couldn't put my finger on what it was or assemble the historical narrative I had come to write. I figured out what happened when, in terms of political events and government policies, from newspaper accounts and political pamphlets. But no matter what questions I asked, nobody related his or her history in a detailed or methodical fashion.

The first time I went to Juchitán, twenty thousand people occupied the town square in protest because the state government had removed the democratically elected leftist mayor from office. Large and charismatic Zapotec Indian women in traditional dress raised their fists in the air, standing up to the Mexican army. I decided to return to Juchitán because there was a story there about fighting for land and recognition, with main characters and passionate scenes. However, while this was indeed the case, during the year Shoshana and I lived in Juchitán the city remained under tight military and police surveillance, and resistance was no longer as tangible as it had been during the big public demonstrations. Politics as something you could hear and see right in front of your eyes had all but disappeared. It was from players in the background as they baked *totopos*, the crisp local tortillas, went to work, and built enormous altars out of flowers that I learned to tell a different kind of story from the one I had imagined. As a foreigner, I was simultaneously rebuffed by this culture and invited in. I was pressed to change my name—to Julio, because people couldn't pronounce "Jeff"—and then laughingly informed that "Jeffrey" is fine because it rhymes with "refri," short for "refrigerator." I was asked slyly about the whereabouts of my wife as I walked through the market and gleefully called *guëro* (whitey) by the sharp-tongued fish sellers, then praised by the flower vendors for my burgeoning Zapotec-language skills. I was mocked in a skit at the cultural center, but when I commented on this afterward to the wife of the center's director, she responded with a pleasant shrug, as if the skit and everything in it were but the dust she was assiduously sweeping before closing up for the night.

I also learned about politics from Shoshana and the midwives whose stories she learned to tell.[3] Joaquina Peral was eighty-one years old when Shoshana and I met her, and she still walked the length and breadth of the town to deliver babies. After a brief introduction and some matter-of-fact questioning, she said she would permit Shoshana to accompany her in her work. At first glance, Joaquina fit the image of the traditional Zapotec midwife, practicing techniques that had been handed down for generations from mother to daughter. But Joaquina's story contained surprises. It turned out, as Shoshana and I learned over Jell-O in her quiet kitchen, that Joaquina was born to a Spanish family in another part of the state. During the Mexican Revolution, Joaquina's parents kept her beautiful sister hidden in their house, afraid she would be raped by soldiers, and finally sent her away to the Isthmus, where there was less fighting. Later, when they disapproved of the man Joaquina wanted to marry, they banished *her* to Juchitán to join her now-married sister. Once there, Joaquina explained with her quick, dry laugh and an elegant sweep of her arm, she asked her Japanese brother-in-law, a doctor, to teach her to deliver babies, to spite her mother.

Joaquina's stories, relayed to me in part directly and in part through Shoshana, who spent whole nights sleeping in a hammock next to Joaquina's awaiting the call to childbirth, changed my notion of what culture is and how political activism happens. Through Shoshana's work, I saw the *work* of culture, the way midwives combined Western medical techniques, local knowledge of childbirth, and Zapotec language and ritual to deliver and nurture babies who would grow up in a cultural world different from that of their parents. As a woman granted entry to an intimate and female space, Shoshana gave me access to a grounded understanding of culture and the mysterious relationship between what happens and what people say. In turn, by focusing on the unevenness of the radical COCEI, its jagged and multistranded character, I could assemble an account of a political movement based in people's daily experiences and stories. I could discern and communicate a movement's internal complexity, its ambiguous position at the borders of many of the things it claimed to defend, such as democracy, nonviolence, and equal roles for women. I could not only understand these attributes but delineate their absence as well, in effect seeing and not seeing them at the same time.

I brought this perspective with me to Brazil, when our family went to live there from 2001 to 2002. I understood, from my work in Juchitán, that what I saw in front of my eyes was always more fraught with conflict than it seemed. And I knew that the big political forces to which we attribute coherence and power are made up of a multitude of individual and cultural experiences, pushing in all directions. Yet if living in Juchitán had made me aware of how complicated things are, what brought me to Brazil was also simple in a way. In a world of growing religious and ethnic fundamentalisms, of elaborate rituals and new religious cults springing up in response to the pains and harms of globalization, ordinary people all over Brazil were doing something utterly conventional that I wanted to believe was still possible.[4] Brazilians were organizing political and cultural movements, such as the Zapotec movement I had studied in Mexico, to improve living conditions in their communities and bring about greater equality and social justice. To achieve these goals, they attended meetings, gathered information, and then came up with out-of-the-box solutions—new ways of protesting in the streets, taking over land, standing up to drug traffickers, and voting in elections. These local efforts strengthened Brazil's democracy from the bottom up, and in the 1990s and 2000s they brought to power national leaders who could successfully begin to combine commitments to economic growth and social welfare policy.

Brazilian activists still held aspects of the imaginary of development that was fostered in the decades after World War II, when people around the globe believed that education and economic development could bring about fulfilling lives for everyone in a pluralist world. If the Brazilian struggles I was studying bore fruit in the twenty-first century, it seemed to me that they could bolster this vision and deepen its democratic and egalitarian components. By making credible the notion that the world as we know it could be re-formed—be rendered just and sustainable—activism in democracy might offer a tangible alternative to terrorism and ethnic wars.

My Mexican lessons traveled well to Brazil. The approach to politics I developed in Juchitán, where radical political leaders wouldn't talk to me, brought me access to Brazilian leaders. When I told them what I had learned from studying a Zapotec Indian movement in Mexico—about the links between politics and day-to-day culture and about studying the margins of politics to understand how things worked—Brazilian activists responded with accounts of the complexities within their own movements. In Porto Alegre, the idea that I wanted to study the participatory budgeting program at its borders, in the places it barely reached, resonated with people's experiences of a political process that empowered local residents but also shaped what they could ask for and constrained what they could achieve. In the southern countryside and in Rio de Janeiro's favelas, my interest in the relationship between culture and politics made sense to people fighting on the frontlines of harsh economic processes, as they struggled to feed their families and keep violence at bay in their communities. They know how movements that claim to support ordinary people—and are in fundamental ways their own—also channel their energies and manipulate them. And activist leaders encounter individuals with their own ways of narrating their lives at every turn.

In 2004, during Emma's and my first research trip as a team, the question no one brought up in Brazil, but that is unfailingly asked of Emma and me in lecture halls, around dinner tables, and in our conversations with colleagues and friends, is how women who started a movement at fifteen by defying their fathers viewed the two of us. They also asked what it meant for us to work so closely together that during lectures and interviews we sometimes finished each other's sentences, and how we managed to carry out a long-term project together. The women we met in Brazil never asked these questions, and it was only later, when we returned in 2007 and started writing a book together, that we began to address them ourselves. During our first research trip, it felt as if people took us for who we were and that the unusual nature of our research team wasn't the first thing on their minds. We wanted to understand what fueled successful grassroots activism so that we could bring that knowledge and spirit home to the United States. In response to our ever-enthusiastic questioning, the women consulted their calendars, chock-full of events and strategy sessions, and brought us along.

We attended women's movement meetings where women discussed every-thing from the workings of the international economic system to the dangers of genetically modified crops, from saying no to their husbands' demands for sex to the need for more dialogue in rural families. We visited small women's pharmacies in the back rooms of farmhouses and union halls and attended statewide assemblies in cavernous auditoriums, learning the movement's songs, listening to lectures, and role playing in small groups. In all of these activities, the conversation could turn on a dime from ordinary tasks and pleasures to the deprivation many Brazilian women confront every day of their lives—isolation, depression, death, and unending work.

We were there when the governor of Rio Grande do Sul refused to meet with leaders of the women's movement, so they bussed scores of women in from the countryside to block off the road in front of the State House. "How do you stand up to the police and walk forward?" was a question the women confronted time and again. We watched a policeman in the capital city push a woman backward and tell her to stay on one side of a line the authorities had drawn in the street, just the kind of treatment the women had been fighting for decades through their meetings and mobilizations. If the woman crossed the line, the officer told her, "we'll send you back home and you'll stay there."

Some of the most revealing moments in our research took place in kitchens as we helped to prepare meals or when we accompanied women on their daily tasks around the farm. It was often in their homes that we learned about the complexity of their lives and the places where activism and daily life come together, where women become activists before they ever attend marches and demonstrations. And where they remain activists long after the most visible successes of mobilization.

During our research trips, Emma and I took a walk each evening, up and down the town's few main streets as we planned our schedule for the next day. Sometimes we interviewed each other as we walked, to figure out what kinds of questions might elicit good stories. And we tried to understand what was different about the way the women we talked to recounted their lives, compared to the kinds of storytelling we were accustomed to in the United States. Why was it hard at first to get to the rough and tumble of conflict inside the women's movement, and within the women themselves? Perhaps it was the power of the movement's own story, linking one event to the next as a progression of achievements, and imagining that once women understood their situations, they would join the women's movement—even though it didn't always work out that way.

One night, when Emma returned to our makeshift office in our hotel, she tossed her bag onto her desk and turned to me, tired yet clearly exhilarated, and asked, "How do you know when to be a real person when you're doing research? When do you express thoughts and opinions and ideas of your own?" Emma's question made me realize that in doing research with my daughter, I brought some of my own life to my research site. Was Emma talking about expressing her own thoughts to others, or to me? Researchers who travel thousands of miles from home generally have the option of observing and engaging in other people's lives without sharing any of their own. But here I couldn't help but be a real person, because my family, my excitement about grassroots politics, and my own thinking about gender came together in Ibiraiaras.

4

GAMBLING ON CHANGE

Emma

For most of her life, when Gessi wanted a law to change, she took over a highway or camped outside the governor's office door. In 2001, her approach changed: she left the statewide women's movement to lead a local health department, and she started contacting government officials from her office in city hall.

I met Gessi in 2001. She stood in front of hundreds of women who had arrived on buses for an annual statewide meeting of the women's movement. Wearing brightly colored movement T-shirts, they watched Gessi crisscross the stage, calling for legal rights and social change with the passion they had come to expect from this militant leader. Gessi had spent the past fifteen years of her life organizing protests in major cities and persuading women who had never left their houses alone to attend women's movement meetings. She met her husband, Didi, when she was organizing farmers in Ibiraiaras, his home-town. Even after they were married, she continued traveling between protests in major cities, meetings in church basements on distant rural roads, and their house in Ibiraiaras, an hour from her parents' home in Sananduva. Her daughter, Natália, born in 1999, saw it all: the long bus rides, the police confrontations, the time the bus broke down and everyone slept by the side of the road.

At the meeting in 2001, Gessi made an announcement that would change her life. Gessi and other leaders had formed a makeshift circle in a dusty clearing between picnic tables and plastic tents to talk about who would lead the movement the next year. Gessi was asked to continue as full-time leader of the women's movement. She said no, because she had accepted a job as head of the health department in her town of seven thousand.

Gessi told me years later that she almost changed her mind when she looked out at her colleagues and friends. Together, they had founded a move-ment other people insisted would fail, then spent fifteen years engaged in the kind of militant, in-the-streets activism they thought would change the world. The movement "was a place I helped construct," Gessi said. She believed in challenging the government from the outside. But she also saw potential in using government resources to bring tangible improvements to people's daily lives, and in joining the institutions so as to make change from within.

Gessi Bonês. *Photograph by Jeffrey W. Rubin.*

"I have two hearts," Gessi said from an office in city hall, three years after she accepted the job in the health department. Since the day she was offered that job, Gessi has wanted to be in two places at once: in the institutions, with the health department, the schools, and local elections, and in the streets with the women's movement, marching and singing with fists raised defiantly in the air.

Citizens and activists across Brazil confront the question of where to *do* politics—in the streets or the institutions or some mixture of the two. The choice Gessi faced in 2001 would have been unimaginable when the women's movement first began. Under Brazil's military dictatorship, citizen participation in the government was out of the question, and for the first decades of democracy, conservative or centrist leadership offered little room for Gessi's radical views. When I asked Ivone why movement leaders decided to take over the governor's office building during the campaign for maternity leave, she told me that "all other doors were closed" to them. Demonstrating in the streets, or, in this case, in the hallways of government buildings, was the only choice for activists who wanted a voice in politics.

In the last years of the military dictatorship and the first few years of democracy, grassroots activism seemed to be the most effective way of ending the military dictatorship and pushing for democratic reforms that would improve conditions for the nation's poor majority. The constitution that was created after the military dictatorship ended in 1985 gave the government the right to carry out land reform, but it wasn't until the MST staged land takeovers that the government began to exercise this right. Many rural women didn't have birth certificates until the women's movement ran buses across the countryside, transporting women to the towns where they could sign up for the documentation that would give them access to newly won rights.

Then doors started to open in government for progressive activists. The Workers' Party began winning elections at national and local levels in the mid-1990s, culminating in the landslide victories of Luiz Inácio Lula da Silva, known as Lula, in the 2002 and 2006 presidential elections. Activists who had fought to bring down a military dictatorship twenty years ago were suddenly able to run for local office and win, or to work in a government department and make actual changes in policy and practice.[1] Two years before Lula took office, a Workers' Party candidate, Ivanir Dode, won a mayoral election in Ibiraiaras. Rather than maintaining the status quo, Ivanir tried to find innovative ways of improving life in his town. In a move that angered many of his political advisors, he asked Gessi, who had left school after fifth grade to lead protests against the government, to run the health department.

Gessi asked the mayor for a smaller job, hoping she could work part time in the government and still lead the women's movement, but he refused. The leaders of the women's movement, Gessi's colleagues and closest friends, were equally firm. In their eyes, a social movement had no place for someone who worked in city hall. If you work in the government, they told her, you are not part of the movement anymore.

Gessi had seen herself as an activist since she was fourteen. But she hadn't received a salary in eleven months, because the movement had no money to pay leaders that year, and she and Didi yearned for a level of stability the movement could not provide. The government had changed since Gessi helped found the women's movement in 1986, and she wanted to take on the challenge of making a place for herself there. "In practice," Gessi told me, "there's no recipe that says, 'do this and this and things will work out.'" We just have to *ir fazendo*, she said. We just have to keep doing, and see where things go.

In 2004, Dad and I visited Gessi in her bright-yellow office in the Ibiraiaras health department. The building was constructed with the same basic materials as local working-class houses: concrete walls, wooden shutters, and no heat even in winters. But the simply constructed building was full of energy. People came with major crises and daily health problems, their waiting-room conversations audible through Gessi's open door. She was rarely alone in her office; doctors stopped by with questions, and patients talked about more than just their medical concerns. Gessi knew the town well, remembered people's names, and understood the challenges faced by small farmers and owners of fragile but growing businesses *na cidade,* in the city.

Portuguese has no word for "town," so a place is called a city as soon as there are a few thousand residents and a central square. In Ibiraiaras, it's easy to run into Gessi's young daughter at the local market with friends, buying a tomato to eat when there are none growing behind her house. There are a handful of small supermarkets, pharmacies, and banks. The church covers the northern side of the central square, and its yellow plaster walls match the colors of surrounding storefronts and houses. Though the dust never quite settles, the buildings have a kind of sturdiness that shines through. Stand on a corner for ten minutes and you see modest cars, a few motorcycles, a truck with three levels of pigs squashed together, a teenage boy and girl tossing a ball, and a tractor winding the corner.

The highest building is seven stories, but most are only one or two, and the way the hills work you can see another level of houses no matter where you are. If you set out walking in any direction, you can make it across town in a few minutes, then turn and see it stretched out before you, houses and wide cobblestone streets with just a few cars. The stones extend for as many blocks as the houses do, then truck tracks continue on reddish-brown dirt roads, weaving through kilometers of countryside dotted with small farms. A sign at the entrance to Ibiraiaras identifies it as the potato capital of the state, and the city also produces large quantities of corn, vegetables, and milk. The line between city and farm life is blurred; most people know each one, and the back-and-forth is much talked about and well known.

For people who live in the countryside, getting to the health department is no easy task. Buses run irregularly, and even families with cars face time-consuming drives on unpaved roads. When Gessi started working at the health department, a building near the center of Ibiraiaras, many citizens had never been there. Gessi quickly realized that to make medical services more accessible, she would have to expand the size of the health department staff and the geographic reach of its services.

Gessi had no medical training, and she didn't know how to run a health department. But after fifteen years in the women's movement, Gessi knew how to organize. She increased the number of doctors and dentists employed by the municipality from two to four, doubling the number of medical professionals who provided free care to all residents. Under Brazil's public health system, called the Sistema Única de Saúde, citizens have a right to free health care, but the quality of that care depends on local health departments. Gessi extended the hours of the hospital emergency room in Ibiraiaras so that people could see a public doctor after business hours for free, rather than paying to see a private one or waiting until the next morning. She hired a psychologist and redesigned the health department and hospital buildings to be more efficient and family friendly. Several days a week, she sent a doctor, a dentist, and two medical technicians on a bus to see patients who couldn't make it into town.

Gessi's new programs required resources Ibiraiaras couldn't provide on its own. Federal funding for improving municipal health-care services was already available, Gessi explained, but "you have to go after it." As part of Brazil's universal health-care system, municipalities that take part in a national family health-care program are eligible for funds to hire doctors, nurses, and technicians, as well as *agentes de saúde* (community health workers) who visit local families in their homes. When Gessi took office in 2001, seven health workers had been hired but were not working effectively. They had never been trained, and their pay was coming out of the municipal budget because the other components of the family health-care program necessary to receive federal funding were not in place.

During Gessi's first weeks in the health department, five to ten community members stopped by each day to speak with her. Once she secured funding for new programs and the changes she made took effect, she began to see upward of forty people a day. They came for help scheduling doctors' appointments, arranging rides to see specialists in Passo Fundo, and making decisions about treatment plans. "As soon as you leave your door open and people see that they have access, the work increases," Gessi said.

Gessi hired ten more health workers, most of whom were local women with only primary-school educations, and put each one in charge of a different part of the city. Watching Gessi teach the health workers how to record their home visits reminded me of something she had said about activism: "The richness of popular mobilization is making people believe that they are capable, that they are more capable if they are organized together." The health workers began making monthly visits to their neighbors' homes to record children's heights and weights, check on chronic health problems, and keep their eyes open for crises ranging from emergency medical needs to unemployment. These home visits, paired with the availability of around-the-clock medical care, had a daily and lasting impact in a place where many people made a living through physical labor and counted on their bodies to stay strong in tough conditions.

Transforming the health department wasn't easy. Neither was making the transition from the streets to the government. When Gessi first entered the health department, her government colleagues asked what someone who had spent her life mobilizing outside official buildings was doing inside one. You have no education, they told her. You only know how to protest and make trouble, so what are you doing here?

"There are people who have been there [in the government] five, twenty, thirty years who don't think as I do," Gessi said. "They say, 'no, I know what I'm doing. Why do you want me to change?'" Changing any aspect of the bureaucracy was time consuming and frustrating after the informal structure of the women's movement. As head of the health department, Gessi once met with a local banker to ask for donations of supplies for a local health fair. As she entered his office, she remembered demonstrating outside the same building years before, demanding better credit for small farmers rather than politely asking for donations. Leaving the building with promises of table-cloths and pens, she missed the dynamism and intensity of running a movement. "In the movement," she said, "everyone worked together. You have a small group of leaders, a collective of women. You sit, discuss, construct, decide, go and do things. Here I feel very alone sometimes. In the most difficult moments, I wonder if it's worth it, if it wouldn't be better to stay in the concrete battle for change." After securing rights to maternity leave and pensions for women across the state, Gessi's focus had shifted to monitoring the health of Ibiraiaras's seven thousand residents. Her work hadn't gotten easier, but sometimes she wondered if it mattered as much.

For Gessi, making decisions about one person was often harder than telling protesters to stare down the police. She told me this in 2004, three years after joining the health department, and I realized then how deeply she had invested herself in her new job, and how seriously she took the work of reforming the department and delivering better individual care. "I think that despite the challenges, we've spent our time here trying to make the government into an instrument of change," she said. "Not all activists agree, but I feel good about what we've done. People joke with me, saying, 'Next year there's going to be an election. You'll continue as head of the health department?' And I joke back: 'No, I'm running for mayor.'"

I don't know if Gessi actually considered running for mayor, but she had certainly gained confidence in her ability to make change from a government position. For the first time in her life, Gessi had a voice in government without having to fight for it, and she had seen how far well-used resources could go toward addressing basic needs like medical care. What's more, with her government salary, she could pay for her two-year-old son, Davi, to attend daycare, and she and Didi didn't have to worry as much about money for food.

Gessi was ready to keep going in the government. But since she held an appointed rather than elected position, she could only keep her job if the mayor who appointed her was reelected. "I never thought I'd be sitting down to plan a campaign," Gessi laughed, and then she did exactly that. One summer when I was there, in 2004, she ran campaign meetings and gave presentations in drafty buildings on the outskirts of town, outdoing even the mayor in her enthusiastic descriptions of the administration's past successes and plans for the next four years. After fighting against the military dictatorship in the 1980s, she was now engaged in the daily work of democracy, betting once again that this path would pay off.

In the midst of the campaign for local elections, I asked Gessi to do a filmed interview for the curriculum Dad and I were designing, and she introduced herself on camera as the head of the health department in Ibiraiaras and a leader of the women's movement. She claimed both identities, hoping, as she had when she first accepted the new job, that she could be both. But Gessi's attempts to live in both worlds—to support the women's movement and make a place for herself in the government—was met with hostility from both sides. Gessi eventually won the respect of local government officials through her careful monitoring of the health of each person in town. She was accepted in the health department, but to her colleagues there—and to leaders of the women's movement—succeeding in the government meant leaving behind her identity as an activist.

In 2001, when Gessi first argued with other activists about her decision, and in subsequent years, when they had stopped talking to each other but continued to voice their opinions to me, various factors entered the conversation: activists' hopes for women in Brazil, their past experiences in social movements, their families' needs, their friendships, and their willingness to bet on new ways of making change. It was hard to tell which factor had been most important in a given moment, and I don't think the women knew for sure. The line between the streets and the institutions, and between activists' personal lives and political visions, was never neatly drawn.

The women with whom Gessi had founded the women's movement in 1986 knew Gessi was making a difference during the years she spent meeting with doctors, negotiating tablecloth donations for health fairs, and making follow-up visits to rural teenagers' homes. But they believed that Gessi should be fighting for major economic changes at the national and international level instead of working to improve individual children's lives. Like many activists who have chosen to stay in social movements even as they are offered positions in government, these women are not content to fight for social services without simultaneously fighting against the system they believe creates and perpetuates poverty, hunger, and inequality. In order for change to occur, they believe, the system itself needs to be transformed.

In line with this vision, Loiva Rubenich and other movement leaders joined forces with activists across the country in 2003 to form a unified national women's movement, the Movement of Peasant Women, known as MMC.[2] As a center of rural women's activism since the 1980s, Rio Grande do Sul was chosen as the location for the national headquarters. The movement also formed a close alliance with Via Campesina, an international coalition of rural movements with a tradition of disruptive civil disobedience. Shortly after the national movement was created and the alliance with Via Campesina solidified, activism in Rio Grande do Sul took a new form. On International Women's Day in 2006, in a protest against the large eucalyptus plantations that activists believed were destroying forests and family farms, the movement occupied the state headquarters of the agricultural giant Aracruz Inc. and destroyed genetically modified crops. In destroying equipment and plants, the movement broke the law and pressed the limits of permissible civil disobedience. Their action engendered harsh searches and interrogations by the police, as well as lengthy legal proceedings against leaders of the movement, some of whom initially went into hiding. It also widened the gap between leaders like Loiva who had stuck with the organized movement's vision of systemic change, and those who, like Gessi, had chosen to focus on improving the lives of citizens in their towns.

Leaders of the women's movement argued that investing in incremental reform meant limiting yourself from the beginning, and that when Gessi joined the health department, she took on the task of governing at the expense of truly reforming the world. They pointed to President Lula, whose election was the culmination of years of hard work and high hopes on the part of progressive activists across Brazil. Instead of taking on hunger and inequality in the bold way many of his supporters had envisioned, Lula complied with the economic policies of the International Monetary Fund and focused funds on paying off debt rather than investing in local institutions. In today's global economy, with its focus on free markets and limited government action, Lula's approach left only limited resources for restructuring the economy, investing in social welfare, and redistributing wealth, the goals that Lula championed during his campaign. For many Brazilians, the economic growth Lula achieved, which by the end of his presidency had propelled Brazil to seventh place among global economies, validated his policies, as did his signature social welfare program, the *bolsa familia* (family stipend). But for activists committed to achieving an alternative vision of economy and society, Lula's approach was a great disappointment, a capitulation to the global status quo.

You'll become a different person when you're governing, Gessi's colleagues in the women's movement told her. The logic of the bureaucracy takes over, so you learn to minimize your demands. You'll stop dreaming so big, they said—and no matter how much you achieve, your work can be undone with the next elections.

In the 2004 interview in which Gessi introduced herself as head of the health department and a leader of the women's movement, she joked that she shouldn't go back to the movement headquarters because they might persuade her to return, and she didn't have time to lead a women's movement.

But we both knew she might not be welcome there. Activists who stuck with the women's movement rejected the very flexibility that Gessi embraced.

From the movement headquarters in 2004, Adriana Mezadri, whose father had once uprooted her organic crops, said the movement didn't "train Gessi to work in the government," it trained her to lead. In the eyes of movement leaders, Gessi, a militant activist and a dear friend, could do more by staying in the movement and demanding systemic change from the outside. Taking the argument a step further, to a place that was harder for me to understand, Adriana told me that if the term "movement" were used more broadly, if the movement took place inside government offices as well as outside them, "it just wouldn't be a movement anymore."

The decision to reject government work as a viable political strategy has grounding in Brazilian history. In a country with a history of dictatorship and corruption, the idea that government would actually improve people's lives seemed to many activists more implausible than plausible, even in the twenty-first century. At first I thought movement leaders just weren't willing to take the risk of supporting Gessi's work in the government, but then I realized that they had spent their lives betting that meetings and mobilizations would bring about real change. They recognized the value of Gessi's work, but in their eyes too much was at stake in the movement's vision of political and social transformation to allow movement leaders to be compromised by institutional goals. Adriana didn't say Gessi's strategy wouldn't work. She said she didn't know for sure what the future would bring, but that the movement wasn't "willing to gamble on that path"—the path of transforming the system from within.

"When they make your life hell, you leave," Elenice Pastore said when my dad asked why she left the women's movement. Elenice joined the movement when her father forced her to quit school after eighth grade, and by 1989 she had a full-time, paid job as a regional coordinator. Working for the women's movement gave her the courage to stand up to her father. She moved away from home to live and study in the towns where she worked, ending the days of early morning walks to meetings and dependence on her father for bus fare. She completed high school in 1992, then attended college in Passo Fundo while working at the movement headquarters there. In 1999, when the progressive state government invited the women's movement to nominate a member to its new commission on gender, leaders chose Elenice. She spent the next three years working to represent movement interests in the state capital, Porto Alegre, where she was also able to enroll in a master's program in sociology. She returned to Passo Fundo in 2002, planning to finish her thesis, which examined women's role in production on family farms, and continue working for the women's movement.

There wasn't a big fight or a single moment when Elenice was pushed out. Upon her return to Passo Fundo, she started hearing about meetings of the movement leadership to which she hadn't been invited, and by the time she found out, the meetings had already happened. "If you make it so that people don't know that something is happening, you push them out a little more each time," she said. At the meetings she did attend, Elenice felt as if there was no place for her anymore. She had studied gender in graduate school, and movement leaders had encouraged her to represent them in government, but it didn't seem like there was a place in the movement for what she had learned. "It was so hard, so uncomfortable," she said, "to have to participate in meetings where you feel so bad."

Vera Fracasso left the movement in 1997 after getting involved in running the local farmers' union. Though Vera and Gessi had fought for union reform as teenagers, by the 1990s, many leaders of the women's movement saw unions as an institution more similar to the government than to social movements. These leaders opted to support a new farmers' movement that was affiliated with the MST, and they didn't see a place in the movement for someone like Vera, who believed the existing unions were a viable way to create change. Vera wonders if maybe she should have fought back: "The decision I made, and other women made, was to distance ourselves from the women's movement. And it shouldn't have been this way. We should have gotten together to have more of a debate within the movement." But what happened, she said, was that "women who thought differently started to be seen differently," and they left.

Vera and Elenice don't know why they didn't fight back. Vera thinks it has something to do with power, with how hard it was for her and other women to "understand what power is and who can exercise it," to see themselves being pushed out of the movement and to claim the right to fight back. They didn't want to turn the movement they had fought so hard to create into a struggle over control. "For fifteen years of our history, we suffered a lot to create the movement," she told me. In 2004, after she had become the first female president of the farmers' union in her town, she still wondered if leaving the movement had been her only choice. "Construct another one?" she remembers thinking when it was clear there was no place for her at movement meetings. "Were we going to have to start all over again?"

Elenice thinks that having so much at stake personally in the movement made it hard to fight back when she felt herself being pushed away. Her best friends were in the women's movement. Male activists, she imagines, might have resolved things through political procedures, such as voting or competing campaigns. But she didn't want to challenge her friends, and she didn't want to weaken the movement she had helped create.

Gessi's health department was dismantled when her administration lost the local election to a conservative party in October of 2004. Many of her colleagues began looking for new jobs the day after the election. Gessi stayed in her position until the last day. "I left the day the mayor left," she said. "Every day when I walked down the road to work, people stared at me and said, 'Ah, but what are you going there for? A new mayor was already elected.' And I said, 'No, until December 31 it's us.'" Gessi put all her energy into the health department until her replacement took over and let her projects fall by the wayside. Gessi saw firsthand that the hard work of incremental reform can be undone with the next elections. She again faced a moment of decision: go back to the women's movement, or continue to forge an increasingly uncertain path within the institutions?

Something about working in the government had grabbed Gessi. Some combination of the concrete changes she had been able to make, the new programs she had helped create, and the stability she had achieved in her personal life made Gessi decide to stay. She hadn't given up on the idea of a women's movement that could include women who protested for rights outside city hall and women who created meaningful reform from within. But she didn't want to rejoin a movement that defined itself in such a way that it "wouldn't be a movement anymore" if it made space for her, someone committed to changing the world but willing to do that in seemingly small ways.

When I returned to Ibiraiaras in 2007, Gessi brought me to a building in the center of town where she had helped start Quitanda, an organic market run entirely by women. "It's a necessary space to have," she told me, referring to the large room where products were sold, "but there's no certainty about how long we can keep it," because the cooperative could run out of money, or the next mayor could take the space away. A moment later, she added, "But who says we need that certainty?" In Gessi's eyes, fighting to change the world is a gamble from the start, and no one on the streets or in the institutions knows for sure how things will play out.

5

FIGHTING FOR RIGHTS
IN LATIN AMERICA

Jeff

In Latin America in the twentieth century, people came on the political scene in a new way. Not only did real people, working and poor and hungry people of all colors, make claims to the economic and political rights of citizenship, but some national leaders began to recognize those claims and redefine national identity to reflect this. At times from the colonial period through the nineteenth century, ordinary, often poor, Latin Americans—peasants, small farmers, Indians, domestic servants, women, slaves, blacks, factory workers, unemployed youths, students, small artisans, and shopkeepers—were able to stir up trouble or make themselves heard, but they were not recognized as having a right to political voice and equality. The running of the nation and the enjoyment of its economic benefits, from capital cities to the smallest town halls, were the province of elites.[1]

This changed dramatically when mestizo peasants took up arms in 1911, bringing revolution to Mexico and overturning the oligarchic status quo. The new postrevolutionary government would henceforth speak for the rights and needs of Mexico's poor peasants and workers. And in the 1930s and 1940s, the Mexican government redistributed more land than any other government in the Western Hemisphere before or since. President Lázaro Cárdenas supported peasants in protecting their newly acquired land, upheld the rights of workers against factory owners, and expropriated the extensive holdings of U.S. oil companies—though these gains were undercut from the beginning as Cárdenas insisted on centralizing political control in his own hands and stifling the autonomy of labor unions and grassroots peasant organizations.[2]

In the decades following the Mexican Revolution, ordinary people in Latin America made their voices heard in country after country, making claims to economic and political rights and having those claims recognized. In general, these efforts were less violent—and the results in national policymaking less comprehensive—than in Mexico. But across the hemisphere, grassroots pressures and prescient leaders brought the claims of those previously excluded to center stage. In Brazil, black culture became a central component of national identity in the 1920s, as samba became respectable and celebrated and promi-

Women's movement demonstration. *Photo by Noraci Debona; used with permission.*

nent artists and scholars identified racial mixing as the backbone of the country's strength and creativity, positions taken up on radio shows and carried far and wide across the immense nation. These were startling turnarounds in a country that had held slaves until 1888, longer than any other nation in the hemisphere, and marginalized Afro-Brazilians immediately following abolition. As Brazil began to modernize in the 1930s and 1940s under the dictator Getulio Vargas, factory workers gained access to a Brazilian social-welfare network and were recognized, despite poverty and lack of education, as citizens. Like the freed slaves, however, they were citizens with strictly circumscribed political rights and clearly defined social roles.[3]

In Argentina in the 1940s and 1950s, Juan and Eva Perón welcomed the *descamisados,* the shirtless workers of Buenos Aires, from the outlying districts to the city center. In a massive demonstration in support of Juan Perón, as workers streamed by the astonished residents of the fashionable downtown, a student perfectly captured this entry of the people on the scene: "From where did they come?" the student wondered. "So they really existed? So many of them? So different from us? Had they really come on foot from those suburbs whose names made up a vague unknown geography . . . ?"[4] The Peróns raised wages, promoted equal pay for women, and created vacation colonies for workers, even as they closed down newspapers and silenced opponents to maintain power.

In the years following World War II, military and civilian modernizers across Latin America envisioned national economic growth that would include all citizens in a modern and materially secure future. Promises of participation and economic security were more rhetoric than reality, but the words were powerful. Almost everyone had a *right* to political voice and a decent material life as members of the nation, leaders stated in one place after another in the middle decades of the twentieth century. However, there were no legal procedures to guarantee these rights, and material benefits reached only a fortunate few among the masses. In an autobiographical account of life in a Brazilian favela during the 1950s, Carolina Maria de Jesus, a poor black woman, captured the feelings of hunger and deprivation that characterized millions of Latin Americans. In her diary de Jesus wrote on her daughter's birthday: "I wanted to buy a pair of shoes for her, but the price of food keeps us from realizing our desires. . . . I found a pair of shoes in the garbage, washed them, and patched them for her to wear. I didn't have one cent to buy bread."[5]

In the 1960s and 1970s, as impoverished peasants flocked to the cities and shantytowns expanded on the outskirts of every urban center, ordinary Latin Americans worked anew to improve local conditions and press for national reform. Inspired by the rhetoric of their own governments and by activists in their neighborhoods, Latin Americans were also motivated by moments of encouragement from the United States, first with President Franklin D. Roosevelt's Good Neighbor policy during World War II and later through President John F. Kennedy's Alliance for Progress, which was conceived to fight communism by simultaneously fostering socioeconomic reform and training police forces.

In one of the best-known examples of successful pressures for reform in the 1960s—and the democratic means increasingly used to achieve it—Chilean peasant and worker organizations pushed Christian Democratic President Eduardo Frei to undertake reforms that he called a Revolution in Liberty, which included redistributing land in the countryside and expanding labor rights in the cities. These reforms were deepened and transformed when Salvador Allende won the subsequent presidential election in 1970, on a platform of more radical change. Pressed forward by a new generation of educated and empowered workers and a coalition of progressive political parties, Allende altered the economic and political rules of the game—prerogatives of ownership, procedures for decision making, levels of wages, and provision of basic services—to improve the lives of ordinary Chileans. Allende's policies turned Chilean society upside down, legally and democratically. Shifting social and economic norms is both a prerequisite and a result of what it means for poor or marginalized people to gain equality.

To cite one striking example of change, while Allende was successfully campaigning for the presidency in 1970, workers at the Yarur Mill, Chile's star textile factory since the 1930s, managed to form a union that was completely independent of management.[6] The younger workers in the factory were better educated than their older counterparts and had come of age as second-generation workers in politically aware neighborhoods of Santiago. To win the union battle, they had to convince the factory's older workers, who had seen their own efforts at unionization in previous decades met with military occupation and mass firings, to again risk their lives and livelihoods to seek better working conditions through legal means. The historian Peter Winn, who interviewed the workers and recorded their histories as these events were unfolding, describes the euphoria, the world-turned-upside-down sensation, experienced by the workers when they formed an independent union and went on strike, shutting down the factory: "I didn't consider it a strike, I considered it a fiesta, a carnival," a middle-aged woman told Winn. "I considered it the most marvelous day in the world, because I said: 'At last, people have opened their eyes and realized what is happening here.' And with that I felt happy."[7] Several days later, Allende's government legally expropriated the factory from its authoritarian owner and turned it over to the workers to run.

To be fully a citizen is to have a voice, to make claims, and at times to join with others to change the world. As activists in Latin America made use of new democratic mechanisms to promote real socioeconomic reform—and stirred people up in the process—military officers staged coups in country after country, with the support of the business elite, landowners, and parts of the middle class. The militaries acted with the explicit support of the United States and the police forces it had trained. This occurred first in Brazil in 1964, when military leaders overthrew the civilian president, Jōao Goulart. For twenty years, one Brazilian general turned over the presidency to another, exercising strict control over all forms of political activity and economic policymaking. And in Chile in 1973, General Augusto Pinochet overthrew Allende's democratic government and ruled with brutal repression for twenty-five years. By 1976, when the Argentine military seized power in their now infamous dirty war against a wide swathe of their country's civilians, all but a small handful of nations in Latin America were firmly in the grip of right-wing military rule. The generals in these countries presided over the closing down of legislatures, the torture and disappearance of activists (with particular physical brutality toward women), and the annihilation of Indian villages. Military governments annulled labor rights, outlawed and persecuted unions, instilled fear through near-random slaughter, welcomed foreign corporations, and emphasized women's domestic responsibilities as wives and mothers. In effect, they constructed a late-twentieth-century version of the oligarchic and patriarchal status quo of a hundred years earlier, promoting economic growth by attacking basic civil liberties. It is hard today to remember back to a time when Latin America was marked by such darkness and violence, with no end in sight.[8]

In the national drama in Latin America, the citizens of each nation were policed and silenced from the 1960s to the 1980s. "When the Yarur workers returned to their jobs on September 20, 1973, Winn writes, "they found their mill occupied by soldiers and run by the army."[9] Winn describes the return of the hated and feared boss, Amador Yarur, to the Yarur Mill—handed back to him by Pinochet immediately after the general seized power—through the experiences of a thirty-year-old activist who lost her job, her home, and her husband to the coup: "But worst of all, they have killed my dream. . . . It was such a beautiful dream."[10]

Today the people are mobilizing in Latin America for a second time, in a new way. Since the early 1980s, spurred by the resistance to dictatorship from a wide range of social groups who had been harmed by military rule or found it stultifying or wrong, almost all Latin American countries have moved from military rule to democracy.[11] And new forms of social movements, community associations, and electoral competition are flourishing.[12] People such as Gessi and Vera and the women in the MMTR initiated what has now been a twenty-five-year effort to reform their societies the hard way—through day-to-day, grassroots politics; through activism in the streets and participation in elections; through movement meetings and moving into the formal institutions of society and government.

However, there is a harsh paradox, and this paradox produces the explosive politics we see today. While people in Latin America now have an unprecedented level of democratic political rights, more of them than ever before are poor. As democracies have endured and even flourished, Latin American societies have followed closely the prescriptions of the leading international banks and continued to be the most unequal societies in the world.

Brazilians and other Latin Americans have rights to speak, vote, and hold leaders accountable, which they rarely possessed in the earlier decades of the twentieth century. And these rights have been gradually, if unevenly, extended in practice, as people have claimed them and acted on those claims. Today a larger percentage of Brazilians vote, with fully secret ballots, than ever before, and elections are more efficiently and fairly counted than in the United States. But at the same time, there is little room for any government to maneuver within the rules of the global economic game.[13] As a result, Latin Americans today not only have no *right* to economic well-being—democracies today do not speak of such rights—but they also have little chance of gaining the minimum economic security, protection from violence, and cultural recognition necessary to feel full personhood in one's nation, community, and home.[14] That's what movements such as the MMTR are trying to change.

PART II

The Enchantment of Activism

6

HOLDING PARADOX

Emma

Mônica Marchesini makes everything her family eats except sugar, salt, and coffee. The farm where she lives with her husband, Joacir Marchesini, and their four children is five kilometers from the center of Ibiraiaras, and they don't own a car. Mônica relies on erratic buses and rides from neighbors to get into town, where she buys the three items she doesn't produce, attends church, and, when Joacir lets her, goes to women's movement meetings.

Mônica's house is blue, wooden, and weathered. Nestled against her family's fields, the house is framed on either side by the milking shed and improvised plastic greenhouse where Mônica starts and ends her days. She milks the cows and looks after the garden each morning and evening; in between, she prepares meals and cleans the kitchen, makes cheese and bread to sell, and does the laundry. Mônica is the kind of person for whom Gessi, Ivone, Vania, and Vera started the women's movement. Leaders of the movement have, at times, made activism their lives, but Mônica, a movement participant, combines activism with daily life on the farm. The outline of Mônica's life, the farmwork and cooking and cleaning, resembles the life her mother lived. Mônica doesn't want to let that life go. She wants to let go of something more subtle: the belief that women do the housework because that's what women are meant to do.

I saw a photograph of Mônica before I met her. In 2002, the year my family lived in Brazil, Dad drove to Ibiraiaras for a short visit. Ivone accompanied him to Mônica's house to help him find his way on the unmarked rural roads. They spent an afternoon in Mônica's kitchen. It was cold, and Dad left his coat on, but Mônica and Ivone wore flip-flops. Dad took a picture of Mônica holding her daughter, Milena, in her arms. When he showed me the photograph, I thought back to the women I had met a few months earlier, when he took me to women's movement meetings in Ibiraiaras and Sananduva. Mônica didn't look like them. Shadows touched the bridge of her nose and filled the hollows above her cheekbones. She looked like she was carefully considering something far away, and the mix of warmth and concern in her gaze was directed somewhere I couldn't see. Milena looked straight at the camera. Maybe scared, maybe just young. Laundry hung above her head, wool sweaters and jeans turned inside out to dry.

Mônica Marchesini and her daughter, Milena. *Photograph by Jeffrey W. Rubin.*

Dad told me the story behind the photograph. When Dad met Mônica, she was forty and had been married for eighteen years. Joacir had been an alcoholic for longer than that. When he came home drunk, Mônica told Dad, Joacir said, "I'm the one who speaks, and everyone must obey me. I'm the one who has a voice." Even struggling on a small farm, they had enough to live what Mônica called "a dignified life," but alcoholism took that possibility away. Joacir tried to stop drinking several times, then started again right away. Mônica said that living with Joacir's alcoholism was like living with "a war in the family."

That's the image I had in mind when Dad and I visited Mônica's house in 2004. The woman I met surprised me. Mônica was warm and talkative. She brought us into the kitchen and filled our hands with oranges and tangerines. The day was warm for winter, so Dad and I wore fleeces instead of coats, and Mônica wore a women's movement T-shirt and black athletic pants. This time, the shirt hugged her body instead of hanging at her sides. Her hands, worn from farmwork and housework, took over the space in front of her broad shoulders and moved with her words. Milena followed as Mônica led Dad and me through her morning routine, first to the milk shed, then the fish pond, the vegetable garden, and back inside the kitchen.

Milena's bright-pink shirt stood out against the wooden house and deep greens and browns of the fields, though she would have been hard to miss even if her clothes had blended in. The six-year-old barely stopped moving, digging in the dirt, helping Mônica with the cows, or tapping me on the shoulder and then running away, shrieking as I chased after her. Mônica's sons drifted in and out of the scene. Joacir, who was tall and lean with a short beard and the same thick, brown hair as Mônica, followed his wife as she walked us through her routine. He wandered in and out of the conversation, standing with us for a few minutes, then turning to check the storage shed or fish pond. He was listening when Mônica told us that he had joined an Alcoholics Anonymous group in town and had gone several months without drinking. He couldn't make all the meetings—it was hard to get into town without a car—but he went when he could. As Dad and I began preparing to leave, Joacir asked if we could give him a ride to town, then ducked into the bedroom to change for the meeting.

A few days after Dad and I visited Mônica on her farm, we saw her at a women's movement meeting. The photographs Dad took at this meeting capture what I remember. Mônica and Milena are both grinning as if they can't help it, beaming at the camera or at something off to the side that they both see. How did so much change in two years? What made the Mônica I met carry herself with confidence and speak in front of her husband rather than deferring to his word, even as the basic outline of her daily life, the housework and farmwork, stayed the same?

I think the women's movement had a lot to do with the change in Mônica, but not in a predictable way. The leaders of the movement could have said to Mônica, "leave your husband or leave the movement." They founded the movement to fight for legal rights on a national scale and to protest unequal gender dynamics in rural homes. So they could have called Mônica a hypocrite for talking about changing the world at meetings and then submitting to her alcoholic husband at home. Instead, they worked to create a space for Mônica to talk about unfair realities she still wasn't ready to change.

Mônica starts working at six in the morning and rarely finishes before midnight. Most of her neighbors live miles away. Women's movement meetings are the only chances, other than church on Sundays and occasional visits to the store, that Mônica has to spend time with friends, and they were the only places she felt comfortable talking about Joacir's alcoholism when he was at his worst. Breaking into small groups at meetings makes talking easier, Mônica told me. "Then you bring your problems to the larger group. Not as one person's problem, but as a whole group." At home, Joacir often spoke over Mônica or told her to shut up. At women's movement meetings, other women spoke on her behalf. I remember sensing a shift in the tone of a meeting when women broke into small groups. During the morning's lectures and activities, women had listened attentively. The pain came out in small circles in the afternoon. Women spoke about the deaths of husbands and children, of sickness that came from the herbicides and pesticides on the fields, of feeling helpless as they watched sisters struggle with depression. Moving quietly from group to group, I was reminded that these women's lives were filled with a kind of suffering I couldn't fully understand.

Ivone says it drove her crazy that Mônica stayed with Joacir. "She's bringing up her kids to be just like him," Ivone told Dad on the drive back from Mônica's house in 2002. She comes to a meeting with nothing but a cookie for her lunch, then gives her son money to go to a restaurant when he stops by the meeting after school. "I wasn't born to accept things as they are," Ivone said. When her first boyfriend accused her of going out with other men when she was away for the week at a women's movement meeting, Ivone gave him hell. "Okay, from now on, you keep your doubts and I'll go on with my work and my life," she told him, ending the relationship the moment it threatened to compromise her independence. When I picture Ivone then, I imagine her turning away with the same poise and almost unintentional grace she has now, beaded earrings swinging against smooth brown hair, crisp emotion filling her blue eyes.

"We kept telling Mônica to leave her husband," Ivone said, "but she wouldn't go." Watching Mônica put up with Joacir was frustrating for Ivone, and she wanted to insist that Mônica leave. But rather than forcing Mônica to change, Ivone and other leaders learned from her. "I don't have kids, a farm, cows, or alcohol in my life," Ivone said. "I learned what that's like from Mônica. At first, I assumed that Mônica didn't come to some meetings because she didn't want to. Now I know to say, well, things got worse in Mônica's house today." Ivone didn't give up on the possibility of Mônica's life changing, but she learned to be attentive to the constraints Mônica faced. This attention to what women's lives are actually like, and not just what they could or should be, is central to how leaders of the women's movement lead. Like Ivone, they have learned to let women change at their own pace, even though this approach means that things don't change right away, and the changes that do take place are often hard to see.

Mônica's first task of the day is to milk the cows by hand. When Dad and I visited in 2004, she brought us out to the milking shed and sent her oldest son to prepare a bottle of milk for a newborn calf. "The milk is cold," she chided him, but he wandered away, and she lifted the bottle to the calf's mouth. "My mother milked the cows," she told us, "and I carry that tradition forward." Then she said that her husband hates milking. Mônica is hoping to build a new milking shed, one that will allow her to stand up while she's milking instead of crouching in a position that hurts her back. The new system will take more work, but the milk will be cleaner. The same goes for the organic vegetables she grows in the makeshift greenhouse that protects the vegetables from rain. Mônica explained that organic farming is cheaper because you don't have to buy chemicals, but it requires more weeding and attention. "Who does the extra work?" Dad asked. Mônica answered without pause or consideration: "I do."

"I'm working for my children," she said, "so that they can have a life that's different from ours. One with less suffering." Though Mônica makes almost everything her family eats, surviving on small farms is getting harder as agricultural companies develop faster and cheaper ways of producing milk, soy, wheat, and vegetables—the same products Mônica and Joacir sell to support themselves. What's more, Mônica is increasingly aware of the effect of pesticides on her health and that of her neighbors. Though many of them have organic vegetable gardens, they handle toxic chemicals in the fields every day, and the pressure to compete with large agricultural companies makes pesticide use hard to avoid. Mônica told stories of neighbors who had died from cancer, and she talked about wanting to get her children "away from the pesticides."

Closing the wooden door to the milking shed, Mônica returned to the routine of the day-to-day. "I milk the cows every morning and night," she said. "It takes one hour. Then I go inside and make breakfast and start making the cheese." She led us into a room off her kitchen, where a refrigerator held three large pots of milk and a basket of eggs. Every other week, Joacir sells Mônica's cheese at markets in nearby towns. Mônica said she's hoping to start selling milk soon. That way she doesn't have to make so much cheese, and the milk companies "come right to your house. They'll come every day if you have enough." For now, she turns the milk into butter and cheese.

Mônica shut the refrigerator and led us back into the kitchen, where she prepares breakfast, cleans up, and then heats the morning's milk and makes lunch. After lunch, she bakes bread, takes care of the vegetable garden, and, if she's done before it's time to start preparing dinner, helps Joacir in the fields. Milena helps too, but she'll start first grade when she turns seven. Mônica said that she likes having Milena around during the day, but she's looking forward to a time when "Milena is older and can help more." Mônica was standing at the sink doing dishes when she said this. Milena was drawing at the table, Dad and I were peeling oranges to eat, and Joacir was sitting on the couch. We were all quiet, listening to Mônica speak.

"It doesn't have to be girls who help," she continued, right after saying she couldn't wait for her daughter to grow up. "Boys can help too. But my sons prefer to work on the farm with their father. He tells them to help, so they do. They don't listen to me like that." So in the afternoons, the boys do homework at the kitchen table, work on the farm, or watch TV while Mônica prepares dinner. When Joacir gets back from the fields, he joins his sons by the TV. "My husband is tired when he comes home from work," Mônica explained. "He likes to sit on the couch and watch TV. That's his place." She motioned to Joacir, who was leaning back, legs crossed and arms slung over the back of the couch. He cocked his head at us, grinned, raised an eyebrow, and nodded in agreement.

"Don't you get tired?" I asked. Mônica shrugged. "It's not that women have more energy. It's just that when they're tired, they're better at not showing it. They take more pleasure in doing things." It's hard for me to imagine that Mônica enjoys every single task every time she does it. "After dinner, I do everything that still needs to be done in the house," she said. She cleans the kitchen, does laundry, and gets things together for the next day. She goes to bed at midnight or one, then rises at six to milk the cows.

Mônica's statements don't line up, I remember thinking. She's contradicting herself. She just said that both men and women eat meals and track dirt into the house, so they should clean up together, but Joacir's place is on the couch. She said she works through the evening, but that her husband is tired, so he needs to watch TV. She said that she can't wait for her daughter to get older so there's someone to help, even though she has three sons and believes that boys should help too. She criticized herself for staying up so late, and referenced a lecture about the importance of sleep she'd heard at a women's movement meeting, but said she can work even when she's tired.

Watching Mônica wash dishes and talk about her family, it struck me that the contradictory things she was saying were also deeply true. She was saying one thing and doing another, but she wasn't being hypocritical. Mônica lives in this space of contradiction. She hopes for one thing and lives another. This is perhaps what the women's movement in Ibiraiaras asks women most persistently to do: believe in a vision of a different world while living immersed in the reality of this one. Worry about things like pesticides and globalization that they can't immediately change. Hope for one kind of relationship and live with another. Wish husbands and sons would help with the dishes, but do the housework alone.

Dad and I use the phrase "holding paradox" to describe what Mônica is doing when she talks about a vision of the world not yet reflected in her daily life. I first heard this term from my clarinet teacher, Mary Ellen Miller, who used it to describe the tension between the composer's intentions, the written score, and the musician's emotions and reading of the music. There are all these different things going on, Mary Ellen said, and they don't quite line up. There are paradoxes and contradictions in the music that she can't resolve. But instead of simplifying things, instead of dropping her own interpretation of the music to follow the composer's, Mary Ellen holds both at the same time, and lets one interpretation shape the other. I think that's what Mônica does: she holds paradox by fighting for change even as many parts of her life stay the same. Mônica manages to take pleasure in her daily tasks and in her participation in the women's movement, even when she can't replicate the movement's vision of equality in her own home.

Not everyone takes on this challenge. At meetings of the Mothers' Clubs, a government-sponsored program that can be traced back to the 1950s and has branches across Brazil, women exchange recipes, make dinner, and plan outings. The women I met at a Mothers' Club meeting in Ibiraiaras told me that the women's movement was for farmwomen, though we all knew that members of both the women's movement and the Mothers' Club came from rural farms and from the center of town. Club members talked about the importance of finding ways for women to get out of the house, something women's movement leaders grappled with as well. The solution? "We go to the beach!"

Mônica and Ivone are not impressed by the Mothers' Clubs. "The clubs only look inward, not out, not toward society," Ivone said. "Women go [to club meetings] and come back and go on with the same lives. Women in the movement go and come back and their lives continue to change." When I asked a woman in the Ibiraiaras Mothers' Club if there were rights women needed that they didn't already have, she said that things could be different. "But I'm raising my son alone," she continued, "and I'm too tired to go to meetings." I took that to mean that yes, we want things to be different, but no, I won't join the movement. Fighting for change is too hard.

Before women can mobilize for legal rights—before they can even attend meetings—they need to be able to leave the house. Persuading their husbands to let them go is a battle almost every movement woman I spoke to has fought again and again. One woman, Magdelena, prepared for meetings by cleaning the house, putting lunch on the table, and then, at the last minute, telling her husband she had to go into town. She didn't tell him where she was going. "Magdelena was doing everything," Vania once told me, describing a night she spent at Magdelena's house before a meeting. "She made up stories, told her husband lies, and worked twice as much in the house—anything she had to do to get to the meeting."

Sometimes I wonder why these women don't plan protests in their own driveways. "Do Your Own Dishes," the signs could say, or "Stop Here for Permission to Leave the House." I saw members of the women's movement block off a two-lane highway in front of the governor's office in the State House. I heard stories of women taking over the building during the campaign for maternity leave. Why couldn't they use the same strategies to fight the injustices closest to home?

Because home is the hardest place to change, one of my students told me when I raised this question in the middle-school class I taught about the women's movement in South Hadley, Massachusetts. "Your pictures are on the walls," she said. "It's where you live." I repeated the comment to Vania when she asked me if my students understood that activism is hard. Vania took it a step further. She said that even though she's an activist and believes in the importance of shaking things up, she's attached to her home routine. She's used to her partner, Ivone, waking early and preparing breakfast. She's used to doing the dishes together every night. Ivone washes and Vania dries. Even when people ask you to, Vania said, even when you want to, it's hard to change.

Women in the movement have more to lose when they try to change their families than when they fight to change a law. Lawmakers may be more powerful than Mônica's husband, but they have never followed her home. They don't sleep next to her and work on her farm. Sometimes the more boldly Mônica presses her husband and children to help with the dishes, listen to her opinions, or let her go to a meeting, the more they refuse to budge. When Joacir used to come home drunk, he insisted that Mônica keep quiet and follow orders. But even when he is sober, the ways in which Mônica is changing—her increasing willingness to say, in front of him, that men should help with the dishes, and her dogged attempts to attend women's movement meetings—put him on edge.

Once when Mônica ran for the city council in Ibiraiaras, the local leaders of the Workers' Party took the unprecedented step of hiring a maid to work in Mônica's house, so that Mônica could fully join in the campaign. Whenever Mônica returned home, however, Joacir would walk into the house directly from his farmwork, sink defiantly into the couch, and put his muddy shoes right up on the table. Ivone, who told us the story later, interpreted Joacir's gesture: "He was saying, 'You left, you're paying someone else to do your work, but it's women's work, so do it.'"

The maid's presence was temporary—Mônica did not win the position and returned to doing all the housework. But still she has come up with strategies to get Joacir to let her go to meetings. She waits until the day of the meeting, when lunch is already prepared, to say that she plans to leave the house. "It didn't work to say, 'on such and such a day, I'm going to a meeting,'" she explained. "Because if you said it earlier, there'd be conflict until the day of the meeting. Sometimes I chose to stay home. Because there was too much conflict. It just didn't work." Mônica and Joacir share a bedroom, a farm, and a family, and though Mônica doesn't believe Joacir has a right to keep her home, she backs down sometimes because the stakes are so high.

Mônica's daily routine hasn't changed since she was married in 1984. She completes the same daily tasks that her mother did. But the way she approaches her work is different. Standing by the milk shed in 2004, Dad asked Mônica a question that seemed silly until I heard the answer. He asked what she thinks about while she's milking. "I think that this is work I do that can help the family, something that contributes to our income and helps with the family budget," Mônica said. "I think about my family. It's milk for the kids to drink, for the family to drink. And the cheese that I'll make after that. We also make butter that I sell." Mônica didn't say, "I'm doing the work that women have to do." She said that her work makes an economic contribution to her family. Instead of correcting her, Joacir listened, and he let stand this framing of Mônica's daily tasks as real, income-producing work. For the two hours that Dad, Joacir, and I followed Mônica around the farm, Mônica spoke and the three of us listened. Joacir didn't correct Mônica or speak over her, even when she said that she shouldn't have to do the dishes alone and that she hopes the balance of who does the housework in their home will shift.

Changes in how women speak about their work and relate to their husbands are less measurable than successful protests for legal rights. But Vera, a former leader of the movement who has seen both kinds of battles—takeovers of government buildings and tough conversations with her husband and sons—insists that they go hand in hand. "If you change the way people are at home, you change who they are in the world," she said. Ivone once told me that she can see the effects of participating in the movement "marked on women's faces," and I thought of the photograph of Mônica I saw before I met her, and the photograph Dad took while I was there. Mônica told Dad the story behind the first photograph. I'm still piecing together the story behind the second one, behind a woman who carries herself with a confidence I admire, who says things that are both contradictory and true, and who holds the paradox of what her life is against what she hopes it might become.

For Mônica, holding paradox is a challenge, but it is also a source of strength. The contrast between the world she envisions at women's movement meetings and the enduring inequalities in her home gives Mônica a sense of a future toward which she can move. It lets her gamble on the possibility of making change even as daily rhythms seem to stay the same. Mônica goes to women's movement meetings, comes home, and, then, when she can, repeats the pattern again. She is faced each day with what she is fighting against and what she is fighting for. It's no surprise, then, that Mônica is steadfastly committed to fighting for change, and that much of the work of the movement falls to women like her.

Meetings and mobilizations and laws change people, but some parts of families can only be changed from within. When Gessi and Ivone started the movement in 1986, they didn't want women to leave their farms and their families behind. More than winning any single legal right, they wanted—they still want—to change the texture of daily life in ways that endure over time. That kind of change can't be made by leaders alone. By sticking with their families and with the movement, women like Mônica move the movement forward, bringing the activism of leaders like Gessi and Ivone into paradox-laden homes.

7
SIX MEETINGS
Jeff

The meetings of the women's movement often surprised me. They were always different, filled with unpredictable mixes of economic analysis, discussion about gender, and personal encounters. I attended a lot of them and saw that some things remained constant. Women entered the meeting halls with gaiety and a kind of communal grace, even when individually they were shy or shifted uncertainly as they took stock of their surroundings. Arriving in groups from their hometowns, some set their belongings down with a sure knowledge of procedure and schedule. Others paused in the entranceways, turning awkwardly from the meeting space before proceeding to where they would store their bags and sleep, a bare wooden floor in the basement of a church; the concrete bleachers of a gym, just wide enough for a blanket or sleeping bag; or communal tents constructed in no time out of long sheets of black plastic in the sprawling yard behind a union headquarters.

Communal offerings were carefully placed at the front of the meeting area, which might be a small back room in a union headquarters or a cavernous auditorium. These were the products the women brought from their homes or towns: chamomile, beans, potatoes with their roots sticking out, sacks of oranges, a glass pie plate of soil, flowers in vases, marigolds, roses, candles, bread, cheese, a Bible, a painted banner, bananas, peanuts, winter squash, small brown baskets of dill, cloves, anise. Together they formed a live and growing collage, an image of plenty made from everyday ingredients.

Meetings began with songs and were punctuated and shaped by melodies. The songs welcomed you and drew you into the room in a visceral way, as if the musical sounds touched women's faces and in so doing brought public resonance to what had been private experience. "Good morning, my sister, my friend" meant each woman would turn to the woman at her side and at the same time feel herself welcomed. The greetings brought smiles, and the gestures and turning and clapping were a form of playfulness generally absent from harsh farm life. Lyrics like "This is our country, this is our flag" grounded encounters in an incomplete but tangible Brazilian nation. The phrases "To change society, participating without fear of being a woman" and "We make our own history" meant what they said, not dogmatically or insistently, but

Ivone Bonês (*left*) welcomes participants to a meeting. *Photograph by Jeffrey W. Rubin.*

plausibly, as if there were a road ahead and it could be discerned, so that the future took up residence right here in the present.[1]

The main events of the meetings were lectures and communal meals. Lectures about imperialism, lectures about economic threats to family agriculture, lectures about women's health and women's spaces of comfort and discussion, lectures about how women and men were equal until capitalism came, and lectures about how local economic production and distribution could reshape the Brazilian rural economy. The titles of talks and lectures didn't fit their content in any direct way. At the Assembléia Estadual (State-wide Assembly) in November 2001, the first of the women's movement meetings I attended, I looked to the two-hour talk titled "Gender Today" to bring me to the heart of relations between men and women in the countryside. However, what I heard went something like, "Imperialism, through Monsanto's genetically modified crops, is killing our children, and we need to plant natural seeds," which seemed to reduce gender to a discussion of children and nature.

"What is wrong with Brazil?" asked the keynote speaker, Eliana Martins, at the front of the large auditorium as upward of three hundred women listened.

After a cascade of responses from the audience—poverty, hunger, inadequate medical care, farms that can't survive, husbands who see their wives as property—Eliana tied things up in a neat bundle with the conclusion that "we need to look at the formation of Brazil, at a process of colonization that approached Brazil as a business." She proceeded to cover centuries of Brazilian economic history in one long talk. Brazilians have no past to go back to, Eliana explained, they "have only the path to the future," and to get there "you need to clean the window so you can see." What Eliana sees, in addition to the weight of colonization in producing centuries of poverty, is that sustainability is the natural concern of women.

Eliana's lecture was followed, after lunch, by a pageant of bare-chested men and pregnant woman bearing platters of seeds, as figures representing wind, water, and earth led the way. At an open meeting of the executive committee later that day, I listened to discussion about who would join the committee for the next three years, realizing only later that this was the moment when Gessi announced her decision to head the health department in Ibiraiaras and withdrew from her position of leadership in the movement. After some disagreement back and forth, the committee named a replacement, and women of all ages swayed arm in arm, singing with palpable conviction and pleasure of a world without harm. Colorful MMTR T-shirts were sold in a makeshift store, and government officials arrived from Porto Alegre—men in suits and women in loose, elegant skirts and jackets, the sympathizers of the urban Left—to chat, give speeches, and leave. In the evening, after simple dinners prepared with others from their hometowns, the women attending the assembly washed dishes in large vats by the outdoor spigot and let the cooking fires die down. Sitting in circles in the black plastic tents or milling about the darkening yard, they joked about how they would deal with the messes their husbands and children were making at home and wondered together, in response to the events of the day, how they would bring women's needs to their town halls and local health clinics over the coming year.

In this chapter, I describe six meetings that I attended in 2001 and 2002, from the Statewide Assembly in November through a series of International Women's Day gatherings in March. The enchantment of the women's movement, which I sensed at these meetings, isn't produced by their content alone. Rather, enchantment emerges in the mood at meetings and mobilizations, a structure of feeling woven from political analysis, pageantry, and protest over time.

In early 2002, I attended the planning session for the Catholic Church–sponsored event called *Romaria da Terra* (Pilgrimage for the Land). Organized by women's movement activists and Church leaders in Sananduva around the theme "A Land without Harm," the event brought together twenty-five thousand men and women from across the state of Rio Grande do Sul, including the bishop, the governor, and other civic and religious leaders, for a day of lectures, music, and, above all, socializing. In a small *capela* (chapel) during the day of planning for the Romaria a month before the event, the twenty-five or so organizers opened the process by placing their hands around a plate of soil raised high, those in the center touching the soil and the others reaching toward it. The women present were experts at organizing every step of the upcoming event, from the arrival of hundreds of buses and morning coffee to the procession along dirt roads to a central gathering space in the woods, with picnic lunches, displays, speeches, and songs. The planning discussions were spirited and brought clear pleasure to the participants, who worked out, for example, the size of the Bible and the baskets they would carry at the head of the procession. This type of symbol, a priest explained, "has to be exaggerated to work, and the size of the baskets depends on the size of the Bible. If you use a big Bible, then you need big torches and big baskets."

As they proceeded, the planners reminded themselves to take notes, not leaving anything to chance. "We can't depend on the *Espirito Santo* (Holy Spirit); we have to do our part," they said only half in jest. The organizers listened to potential songs for the event—"yes, this one's nice"—making sure religious, women's, and Indian groups were represented in the music. They chose two children, a boy and a girl, to emerge from a giant globe to enter the new world *sem males* (free of harm). Members of the town government arranged for the flag of Brazil, the banners of different local groups, and colorful flags representing civil rights—one for each right—to be ready for the event, noting that "things have to function by symbols as well as words." And the women's movement activists made sure to focus on brass tacks as well, reminding everyone that "the important things at a pilgrimage are water and bathrooms." The same planning group gathered again on the day before the event to clear the meeting place in the woods where the meal and speeches would take place. Teams carted away loose underbrush and set up fences and booths. They adorned the space with palm fronds and plants and vegetables. Many tasks seemed to get done effortlessly in the long day of work, with lots of milling about and a simple lunch of risotto and bread.

It was a day of greeting. I was struck repeatedly in the countryside, where the Catholic Church had stimulated widespread activism, by the culture of greeting, as men and women alike addressed and welcomed one another whenever they met with kisses, hugs, or handshakes, depending on the relationships, and always a direct hello. This in itself was a triumph of Church and civic activism in a place where husbands had long ignored their wives when they entered the room or never called them by name. A middle-aged woman from a small town near Sananduva sold straw hats that she had made by hand, and I bought one that fit me perfectly. A teacher named Paulo and his friends built a model of an organic family farm on one side of the road that the Romaria would follow and, across the way, there was a mirror-image model of an evil farm that was owned by a multinational corporation and used chemical compounds to grow genetically modified crops. There were signs all over the place with directions and explanations, as well as labels on the simple wooden booths that ringed the meeting area.

As we headed home from the day of preparations, Vera, who had as always played a lead role, commented on the hat her female friend was wearing: "That's a man's hat," she said definitively, and I wondered about the identity of my own new hat. Paulo, who was walking with us, saw it differently. "It doesn't matter," Paulo said. "There's no gender in hats." This was followed—at the end of a long day of hard physical work clearing the grove in the woods for the pilgrimage—by a discussion of brim styles in men's and women's hats: bent up for men, I learned, and turned all the way down for women. Then, in the car, Paulo put on a hat. "Is that a male or female hat?" I asked with amusement. Paulo had no trouble answering. "It's masculine," he said. "Because I'm wearing it. Each person uses what's best for him. My wife wears this one, too."

On the day of the pilgrimage, organizers gathered in the large shed next to the chapel at six in the morning to greet the buses as they arrived. Some women stayed in the kitchen making coffee and putting out bread on plates. Hearing that the organizers were worried that there would be nothing happening during the long march between the chapel and the clearing in the woods, where the day's events would take place, a priest assured the organizers, "The symbolism will speak." In the clearing, an orange plastic tarp sheltered the stage, and the priests set a radical tone. "The land should belong to those who work it," Bishop Orlando Dotti stated clearly. "We are against neoliberalism and for the people who work the land." Father Cláudio, who had stimulated the youths of the region to activism, spoke of the grassroots resistance of people who organize themselves. "You can't have justice when leaders are being killed in cold blood and those in power do nothing to prevent it," Father Cláudio told the vast crowd, referring to the assassination of landless activists in the state of São Paulo. And then Luciana Piovesan, a slender and sharp-tongued leader of the MMTR, held the immense gathering in the woods captive as she spoke earnestly into the mike against the bright-orange backdrop. She was more compelling even than the priests, transfixing in her eloquence that the economy of the land must change and women must also change. Luciana, we learned later, was an expert in organizing demonstrations in Porto Alegre; her voice would slice the air and rally support even as the police sought to silence demonstrators.

A young man I met, who was raised on a small farm in Rio Grande do Sul and had worked in the U.S. Midwest on a much larger one, surveyed the gathering, where families of farmers and landless workers from across the state shared elaborate picnics as they listened with an easy attentiveness to speakers and songs. The young man commented on the strength of the grassroots movements in this region of Brazil. I asked, "Why are they so strong?" And he answered, "Because we realized we were producing every-thing, paying everyone for the inputs, the seeds and fertilizers, and then getting nothing for ourselves."

This is what the economic speeches I listened to at women's movement meetings were trying to convey. Lecturers presented narratives of colonialism and the exploitations of the Brazilian economic system in exhaustive detail, and then women responded with incidents from their daily lives, personal accounts of their experiences of subordination and silencing. The lectures seemed to be the backdrop for the outpouring of responses, just as the physi-cal meeting halls were the backdrop for offerings and song. Unfairness—the damnable way the world worked, over and over—and enchantment—the new space of expectation, the hope and even conviction that the imagined future would become the present—formed the twin foundations of activism. The unfairness of the world around them drew these women to activism, and enchantment made their commitments endure.

The next meeting I attended was in Porto Alegre on March 8, International Women's Day, when several hundred women from various rural social move-ments, including the women's movement itself, gathered in the state capital. They met in a public gymnasium, preparing food in tents outside and sleeping on the wide concrete bleachers that wrapped around the giant gym. In one talk, I followed the stages of the *Plan Real* (named for Brazil's currency, the *real*), the economic program pioneered by the former Brazilian president Fernando Henrique Cardoso. In a lecture that lasted the entire day, Milton Viario, a speaker on loan from the metalworkers union, analyzed Brazil's recent economic trajectory in detail: "If eleven million people were unemployed, this was planned." It was hard to see how Milton's explanations of every twist and turn in Brazil's recent economic trajectory would contribute to women's daily struggles. It might be, however, as I realized later after a conversation with Ivone, that what Milton was doing was neither more nor less than imparting information, albeit an amount that seemed to me so specific and at the same time so simplistic in its assumptions as to be indigestible. Receiving information, so copiously and generously given, was a radical act for five hundred women from whom information was usually withheld by fathers, husbands, and priests.

In another talk, women learned from Vanderléia Daron, an MMTR advisor, that for 90 percent of human history, women and men had lived in primitive communes where women played a central role, activities were organized collectively, and there was no social inequality. This lasted, Vanderléia explained, until capitalism subordinated workers and, by extension, women. Cast from this paradise, what did women experience? Upon asking this question, Vanderléia handed the mike to woman after woman, who left theory behind to explain the ways men prevented them from living *uma vida digna* (a decent life).

"I was a slave to my husband for thirty years. Thank God he left; now when I want to leave the house I leave," one woman announced. Another asked the large group, "How many women just work, work in the house and on the farm, how many women keep working in the house, tied to the cows, tied to the children, the husband, never leaving the house?"

"When I was young," another woman, blond and weathered but not old, went on, "men controlled everything on the farm. I was nursing and pregnant and working in the fields, with another child at home. We had to wear long skirts while we worked. We had to work until the moment we gave birth." This speaker showed no signs of pausing, but another woman grabbed the mike: "I'm going to tell you a bit about the struggle, my struggle. My retirement wasn't easy. It was hard to get money for the bus to come here."

Vanderléia had to insist on taking back the microphone to continue her presentation, and she proceeded to condense the women's torrent of descriptive comments into a single explanation. Vanderléia explained that all workers are exploited, that Brazilian society puts women in a position inferior to men at home, and that "we need to fight both struggles together." Then Vanderléia did something remarkable, zeroing in on the need for women's activism in a series of quick rhetorical moves: "If we put down our banners and stay home," she said, "they'll take away our rights." Women cannot rely on their role as mothers: "If we focus on the mystery of creating life, of having babies, of caring for children, then we end up reproducing the existing system." Women need to realize, Vanderléia went on, that "we all dirty the house, women need time for rest and health, and housework is real work. We have to rethink the relationship of men and women in the house, who decides, who makes financial decisions, why we find few women in decision-making positions in the community."

"We can't struggle just for women," Vanderléia continued, shifting instantaneously from gender to economics, from women to men, "because then we come up against class, and we come up against the mask that machismo puts on men. Change happens through an organization of women, but also through the relationships between men and women." In Vanderléia's analysis, the market economy destroyed a paradise of gender equality; in another version, which I heard at a women's pharmacy a few days later, men were so threatened by women's strength that they banded together to subjugate them. As Vanderléia brought her narrative to the twentieth century, she presented an account of Brazilian economic development. Though lacking in nuance, her account offered sensible explanations for the country's record of spectacular industrial and agricultural production and entrenched and abject poverty. Then, after exiting from the front of the auditorium to applause and thanks, Vanderléia turned on a dime and ran back, holding a pamphlet in the air and reading from a list of signs of domestic violence, giving out the name and phone number of an organization where women who were victims of violence could seek help. When I talked to Vanderléia afterward and commented on her last-minute return with the pamphlet, she told that me she just couldn't leave it out, that the Catholic Church wants women to be submissive, but she felt that she had to do it.

The evening entertainment began with a pageant about local agricultural production, replete with platters overflowing with seeds, the subduing of a figure depicting an evil Uncle Sam, and a flower-draped pregnant woman descending out of the bleachers with the ideal family, a husband and child, right behind her. The pregnant woman was young and radiant, with dark flowing hair, her bare-skinned belly bursting forward. This *mística*, as it is called, the artistic and cultural currency of Brazilian social movements, was pioneered by radical nuns and priests and leftist youth as they pulled their communities to consciousness raising and activism in the face of dictatorship. Mística included songs and religious symbols, the enormous painted banners and collages of offerings that set the scene for movement events, pageantry and skits at rallies and meetings, and even the simple exercises that women performed together at gatherings, like squeezing an orange or stretching an elastic band, to show how they themselves were sucked dry and stretched to the breaking point.

Initially, mística was an exotic gift that promised, improbably, a path out of everyday life. In its religious cadences, it sanctioned the space of the women's movement for rural women who might otherwise have seen meetings and marches as far too political and secular. And the concrete manifestations of mística, such as elastic bands and crafts projects, gave women something to take home so they could show their husbands what they did at meetings.[2] Now, after years of demonstrations and meetings, the familiar music and imagery evoke the present as well as the future, enabling women to recognize at once the vibrancy of their collective action and the difference it makes in their daily lives.

Later the same evening, a street-theater troupe put on a play about sexual abuse in families, blaming the abuse on urbanism and unemployment, but focusing squarely on the father poised to rape his daughter, as the mother walked in on the scene and had to respond. The group explored the topic using a technique developed by Augusto Boal in his groundbreaking work, "Theater of the Oppressed," stopping the play and asking the audience to discuss and complete it in alternate ways.[4] The women were hesitant to come up on stage and take the parts of mother and daughter, but the scene was indeed replayed, with cajoling and some help from the few men present, who found it easier to perform in that setting. In the reenactments, the mother protected herself and her daughter first with flight, then with argument and outrage, and finally with violence.

Everything was different at a meeting in Sananduva, where I went the following day, driving five hours into the interior to attend a much more local

International Women's Day celebration, cosponsored by the local MMTR chapter, the leftist town government, and several other civic groups. At this meeting, which also brought together more than three hundred women, imperialism was nowhere to be found, and the focus was on sleeping in the right position. On stage, a physical therapist in high heels, with sunglasses pulled back over her hair, demonstrated the proper way to achieve a restful night's sleep, on her side, with a tennis ball under her shoulder and a pillow between her knees. Other therapists explained how repetitive stress disorders resulted from too much milking or too much harvesting, and they offered the suggestion of breaks, correct posture, and stretching, as well as working at these activities less when there is inflammation. This advice made sense but seemed of limited use in the face of the before-dawn-to-after-midnight daily routine necessary for survival on small family farms. The first therapist concluded her list of suggestions for how women should manage their work by reading a homage to women that described mothers as *administradoras de felicidade*, their families' personal happiness managers.

Next, a male speaker from the Office of Technical Assistance and Rural Extension Services, known as EMATER (Empresa de Asistência Técnica e Extensão Rural), which sponsors Mothers' Clubs across the countryside, spoke forcefully about the harms of pesticides as they get on clothes and into the family laundry, penetrate the earth, and enter the roots of fruit trees and from there the blood and lungs and brain, causing physical illness and depression. The speaker listed specific agrochemicals, the number of liters used on the average farm, and the depth into the earth to which they descend. Two hundred thousand liters of pesticides are used every year in Sananduva, he explained, and the whole world is contaminating itself. To avoid this harm, the speaker counseled women to stay away from the antidepressants now widely prescribed by rural doctors and to use instead the remedies they learned from their grandmothers. He advised them to eat white potatoes, not yellow ones, and not to buy tomatoes from São Paulo. He asked, rhetorically, "Why have we stopped producing brown sugar, right here in the countryside, and instead go to the supermarket to buy white sugar?" He suggested that if everyone used brown sugar, they could support a factory right here in the interior. "The less you buy in the supermarket," the speaker concluded, "the longer you are going to live."

In addition to staying away from the supermarket, women were told that the right attitude was key to being a good happiness manager. A female psychologist began her lecture by asking women what changes they'd like to see in their lives, and women from the audience spoke of having time to themselves, apart from housework and farmwork; understanding their lives, where they come from and where they are going; and escaping physical pain and the negative thoughts that haunt them. The answer, the psychologist said, was to find the opportunity and courage to make changes: "Life is made up of moments that can be transformed into good moments or worthless ones. They are moments that we conquer, that we make." As a first step, women needed to start doing things that give them pleasure: "If you want to change your life, start by planting the seed today, and this will bring your emotional blossoming."

At this point in the meeting, Rosane Dalsoglio, one of the leaders of the MMTR in Sananduva, announced that the women's movement had secured a grant from the state government to set up alternative pharmacies. The pharmacies would produce natural remedies and address women's emotional needs, and basic equipment for the pharmacies (tables, stoves, and refrigerators) would arrive the following week. The various groups of women present —Mothers' Clubs, church groups, the farmers' union, local government agencies, and the women's movement—greeted this announcement with enthusiastic applause, united in their support for the new initiative. In response, Rosane outlined the MMTR's past successes in gaining pensions, maternity leave, and health-care services. She encouraged women to join the expanding movement and visit the pharmacies, which MMTR leaders hoped would bring together self-help strategies, discussion about gender, and continuing grassroots mobilization around economic issues. Following Rosane, the president of the Sananduva farmers' union, Ademir Pertille, summarized the day's lectures with an economic perspective, reminding the audience of the union's fight for a society "where we don't see one side accumulating wealth and the other side suffering hunger and poverty." Ademir emphasized that what Sananduvans need are economic conditions that will allow them to stay on their farms.

Father Fabiano, sweeter and younger and seemingly less committed to transforming the existing world than the previous generation of priests in the region, asked the audience of three hundred women from his parish, "Did you pray already today?" Father Fabiano wanted to know "how many of you have the habit of making the sign of the cross when you get up?" And he asked the women to remember that "so many women, people, mothers . . . have a faith that is capable of transforming mountains. Since creation, women have had an important role, though often it is just Eve's guilt that is remembered." To back up his point, Father Fabiano listed the names of prominent women in the Old and New Testaments. Things can be different, he asserted, but change is only possible if men and women join hands and see each other as equals. He concluded by playing a cassette tape of a man singing, vibrantly, "Partner, give me your hands. I need the love you give me."

The organizers of the meeting in Sananduva proclaimed it a great success, a day of diversion and information for the hundreds of women who attended. The women themselves responded with gusto to the presentations, animatedly conversing over lunch and gathering on the walkways and lawns outside the large auditorium afterward, in no rush to get home. In addition to the lectures, there had been guessing games and jokes that brought laughter at conventionally sexualized gestures and word play—but women were the ones performing and laughing in public—and a play that gently mocked the authority and gender relations in a traditional rural family. When I talked to Vera at lunchtime, she commented on how long it takes to change gender roles in families and how much the women liked the all-day event. Women's fierce need for social activities—and the straightforward way they appreciated lectures and skits and practical advice—had propelled activists in Sananduva to organize such meetings in the first place. It was a day of warmth and camaraderie for women from different hamlets and small towns, and they chatted in groups outside the meeting hall long past Father Fabiano's closing song.

In a church basement in Santa Lucia, a tiny neighborhood just outside of Ibiraiaras, I found what I thought I had come to Brazil and the women's movement looking for, though in the end it was just a small part of the story. The damp and dark room, about three square meters, hugged a grassy hill under an old but well-tended church. From the road all you could see was the front of the church, yellow plaster with blue trim, and a few scattered wooden farmhouses. The air in the basement smelled of equal parts herbs and stone, and I had to adjust my eyes as I entered before I could make sense of the scene. Sheltered from a relentless summer sun, thirty-five women from throughout the region gathered for a three-day course in traditional medicine. The lessons and discussion would prepare the women to run the alternative pharmacies in their towns.

I attended the training sessions with Shoshana and our three daughters during the week following the self-help meeting in Sananduva. I think our time in Santa Lucia as a family had more impact on my ability to do research on the MMTR than anything else I had done to get access to the movement. A meeting is a performance, a backdrop, and a pathway at the same time. Meetings are places, women in the interior told me over and over again, to which they fight to come and where they feel valued, where their voices count. Unintentionally—unavoidably—we performed our family life for women in Santa Lucia even as we thought of ourselves as observers.

I had arrived in Sananduva and Ibiraiaras through trusted intermediaries. Leaders of the MMTR met with me in their headquarters to discuss the objectives of my research and then formally invited me, by fax, to the state-wide assembly. During the interview, I showed them my book on Juchitán, which featured an old Zapotec woman and her young granddaughter on the cover, and explained my interest in social movements and my understanding of the ways that political action was rooted in daily life. At the *Romaria da Terra* (the Pilgrimage for the Land), each new conversation called upon me to explain my presence, to Gessi's in-laws as they picnicked, to her sister when we stopped at her farm on the way home to Ibiraiaras, and to almost everyone I met. Then during the meetings in Sananduva and Santa Lucia, I performed my own husbandness and fatherhood, though I didn't register this at the time. At the Santa Lucia *encontro* (workshop), my wife took notes on the discussions about sexuality, I held fifteen-month-old Esther while seven-year-old Hannah ran among the lunch tables chatting with the young mothers, and twelve-year-old Emma saw a core of political spirit and commitment that has shaped her life and our collaborative project ever since. What I realize only now is that at this meeting the women saw my family and me as we interacted. They saw our daily commotion, the baby crying, her sisters running in opposite directions, Shoshana and me trying to make some order out of the overflowing mix of family needs and meeting activities. Emma watched the women toss their wishes and dreams into the fire in the *mística* that closed the first day of the workshop, and she has remembered that moment ever since. She also remembers this as the only time in her life when I insisted on clearing her plate for her rather than telling her to carry it to the sink herself, so the women would know I was comfortable cleaning up and doing the dishes, tasks I carry out routinely at home. The women watched us and all our imperfections, and it was perhaps something about the nature of my engagement with my family that gained me—and later Emma and me together—entrance. Perhaps the women remember the twelve-year-old girl looking at them as her father looked at her, at her sisters and her mother, and at women speaking their minds in a tight-knit circle.

The woman who ran the Santa Lucia workshop, Rafinha, could have been a skilled facilitator in the Pioneer Valley in western Massachusetts, where I live, down to her well-cut clothes and earnest, soft-spoken demeanor. Rafinha lived on the coast of Rio Grande do Sul and worked with a group of women who called themselves *brujas* (witches) for their knowledge of traditional plants and their critique of conventional Western approaches to gender and medicine. Like the other lecturers at movement meetings, Rafinha had an analysis, a view of how the world worked, that shaped her teaching. But Rafinha held back on tying the pieces together or insisting upon them, and she welcomed the women's voices. She simply identified, with wit and razor-sharp clarity, the ways in which women were subordinated to men.

Rafinha talked with the women in Santa Lucia about sexual intimacy and sexual pleasure, asking them about their own feelings, about how their husbands acted and what their husbands didn't know. She told the group about a twenty-eight-year-old woman who had heard her speak about saying no to a husband's demand for sex. "She came back to see me two weeks later," Rafinha recounted. "She had said no for the first time, and her husband had kicked her, over and over in the hip, until she was black and blue. 'Now I know I can say no,' she told me. 'How so?' I asked. 'I know he won't kill me, he'll just hurt me.'" Rafinha and the women told stories of making special teas to get their husbands to sleep so as to avoid sex, of men saying their wives are frigid because they don't know that women need love and care to become ready for sex: "They don't know because no one tells them, mothers never talk to their boys about sex, and men are more afraid to talk about these things than we are."

The women talked about masturbation—"how could this be a sin?"—and how "no aunt or mother ever said to us, this is a normal, healthy thing," so that they, in turn, did not speak frankly to their own daughters. And then there was their own guilt about this to reckon with, why didn't they know or speak openly? "What are we so guilty about?" Vania asked, and suggested that much of this guilt came directly from the Catholic Church. The gender differences that women identified were stark ones. "Why is it that girls can serve others when they are nine years old and boys are still being served when they're seventy?" These familiar roles shaped ideas about marriage from the start. "Whom do boys dream of marrying?" Rafinha asked rhetorically. "A princess? No, a maid." Then they imagine, "she'll do everything I want, make me all I want." And women play into this, perform it as mothers, neighbors, grand-mothers, godmothers, aunts. Why do boys start being macho? "Because they grow up thinking they are the center of the world, because their mothers don't even get to move their bowels properly because their little boys need them."

"We're afraid that our husbands will love us less if we don't serve them properly," Rafinha continued. "We fear that our sons won't love us enough. We're afraid of feeling useless and of being less loved. Some men, after forty years of marriage, don't know where the towels are kept." And what are penises to Rafinha? "*O bom humor de Deus*" (God's joke). "It's not that genitalia isn't important," she added, "but it's not everything." More than sexual relations, "We need men to be friends and not bosses. We need to eat bread together."

The exercise that made the biggest impression on me at the workshop was about the language in relationships, and it got to the heart of the process of negotiating radical change. What words do you use, the women wondered, when you want to discuss with your husband your desire to go to a meeting? If you don't want to ask permission, and you don't want to say, essentially, "I'm out of here," then what are the words you say and in what sequence? The fact that there was no clear answer to this question underscored the precarious-ness of what the women were attempting. Using language to change intimate power relations brought them to a place of uncertainty, where they didn't always know the right words or gestures. It takes a lot to bring up a subject without the confidence of words and what those words represent. Women get stuck in the argument about leaving the house and preempt it with all sorts of strategies, from preparing several days' worth of meals in advance to waiting to mention their plans to leave until the very last minute. Otherwise, they risk finding themselves in a place they can't get out of.

On the second afternoon, the women broke into groups to perform a series of skits on the topics of the traditional rural family, the modern family, and the ideal family. I was included in the group performing the traditional family, and the exercise began with discussion. At first the women said things that seemed to contradict what I'd heard about life in the past; they remembered it as a time of more socializing. Elena Sgarbossa, an activist of Gessi's generation, talked about the absence of contact in families today, with everyone going his or her own way. Before, she suggested, there was no television and people talked: "I remember my father returning from the fields and praying with the family." Another woman added: "There was a small chapel in my mother's house; my mother would bring over her stool and we would pray together. Now we pray alone." "There was more time left over then," Elena said, "even if there was a lot of work, even if society was more macho."

In the skit, however, the traditional family wasn't idealized. Edenis volunteered to be the mother and asked, "What do I do?" "Everything that the father tells you to do," Elena answered instantly, asking next, "Who will be the father?" "Someone who likes to give orders," another woman suggested, and Elena took up the offer. "So," Edenis continued, "I'll tell the children to do what the father says or he'll be angry." "My mother-in-law is still like that," Elena responded. "She serves my father-in-law, and while he eats, nobody else eats."

In the play, the children all woke up and entered the kitchen to receive our parents' blessing. The father told everyone what she or he would do that day, then left the room first. The process was reversed in the evening, beginning with a silent meal, then with everyone praying on their knees to God the all powerful, receiving parental blessings, and going to bed. After the skit, the women made a list of the negative characteristics of the traditional family: submission of women, obedience of children, oppressive power of the father, absence of dialogue, mothers who reinforce machismo, absence of freedom, macho sexuality, and discrimination against women. On the positive side: large families, parental blessings, family prayer, and no television.

In the modern family, everyone wanted money, and the parents gave the callous children, played flawlessly by young women attending the workshop, all the consumer goods they asked for. The women identified with this urge, which for them caused a painful dilemma. "Our kids want to have the same thing as other kids, but we don't have enough to give them," one of the women lamented. "They want a particular brand, like Nike, that costs 180 reals, that would keep a family going for a month," Elsi added. "This is what we live. It's difficult to say to kids, eating is more important than the brand, if we buy this, we'll be without food or clothes or medicine."

At the core of the ideal family was kindness and dialogue. Children were greeted with kisses, and family decisions were made jointly. The husband prepares a *chimarão*, the intense maté favored by southern Brazilians, for his wife, calls the children in for breakfast, and sets the table with them. They talk about the current project of the women's movement and about finding the resources for the oldest child to go to university. One of the children, who works on the farm, says that his organic garden isn't going well, and he needs help. The father responds, "We'll all come home early to help." All this in the morning!

Each person washes his or her own breakfast dishes, and everyone says goodbye to everyone else. One of the children returns early to help his mother with lunch, and during the meal the gathered family members discuss each person's morning. How was class? A little difficult. How was school? Great, lots of participation. When the father presents an idea for a family project, he asks what the others think.

In the discussion that followed the skits, many of the women said that there wasn't dialogue in their families today.

"Dialogue," Elsi observed, "is when people make exchanges; I say what I think and you say what you think."

"That can be a negative thing," Inez countered, "if we disagree."

"That's okay," Elsi answered, "discussion isn't always calm, there can be arguments."

"We have to experiment with dialogue in our own families," another woman suggested, leading Rafinha to add, "It's not easy to know what dialogue is, you have to learn it as you get older."

Listening to these observations about dialogue, I realized that when women in the movement think about challenging submission and silencing, they envision not equality or independence but dialogue. Dialogue is what they most want, and it is also what they may least know how to do, especially the part of dialogue to which Elsi referred, which may involve argument or anger, conflict or underhanded tactics. Rural women in Rio Grande do Sul have no experience of rough and tumble political deliberation, which some men have gained through work in unions and city councils. The Catholic Church, which mobilized women in the 1980s, maintains itself through hierarchy and order, much as rural households do, with each person carrying out an assigned task. The MST, which galvanized the rural poor of Rio Grande do Sul to radical forms of civil disobedience, similarly runs on a centralized and hierarchical social model, where discussion is controlled and leaders make decisions.[3]

To gain a voice and exercise that voice through dialogue; to figure out what words to say to negotiate with your husband about leaving the house; and to hammer out a common strategy in a women's movement filled with strong and principled disagreement—these were daunting tasks for women in the movement, tasks for which they had no preparation from church, politics, or family life. At meetings they experimented with discussion, step-by-step over years, as lectures gave way to free-flowing comments and exchanges of ideas. Women also faced harsh limits when they could not achieve their goals of inclusiveness and effective strategizing through discussion and voting, and some women left the movement or took paths that divided it. And the same was true at home, where women could press the boundaries of the conventional in unprecedented ways, only to encounter moments of silence and refusal.

What struck me about the women's movement meetings was the way they brought together so many different elements, such as intimacy and consumerism, healing and the history of Brazil. They accepted the value of personal efforts at self-help, but stressed the constraints of the national and international economy, of cultures of the past and of the wider society. At the workshop in Santa Lucia women broke habitual silences to discuss sexuality and gender and violence and the subtle and not-so-subtle forms of domination embedded in their lives. They confronted, with laughter and frankness, the importance of touch and the heavy hand of capitalism, along with the sexual functioning of men and women, the embarrassments and possibilities. Skits enacted the mythology of the past and irresolvable tensions of the present, along with an image of the future made somehow tangible through performance. And that simple exercise, how to discuss with your husband the subject of leaving the house, broached something deep and focused about gender and how to begin to change the seemingly unchangeable.

Luciana Piovesan addresses twenty thousand rural activists. *Photograph by Jeffrey W. Rubin.*

Ceremony at women's pharmacy meeting. *Photograph by Jeffrey W. Rubin.*

Farmhouse. *Photograph by Jeffrey W. Rubin.*

Downtown Ibiraiaras. *Photograph by Jeffrey W. Rubin.*

Inelves Dalmoro and Ivone Bonês at the Romaria da Terra. *Photograph by Jeffrey W. Rubin.*

Elenice Pastore. *Photograph by Jeffrey W. Rubin.*

Mônica Marchesini in her kitchen. *Photograph by Jeffrey W. Rubin.*

Mônica Marchesini and her family. *Photograph by Jeffrey W. Rubin.*

Offerings from home block a street in Porto Alegre. *Photograph by Jeffrey W. Rubin.*

Didi Benedetti at a women's movement statewide assembly. *Photo by Douglas Mansur; used with permission.*

Adult education class. *Photograph by Jeffrey W. Rubin.*

Community gathering. *Photograph by Jeffrey W. Rubin.*

Ivone and
Gessi Bonês.
*Photograph by
Jeffrey W. Rubin.*

Farm family at home. *Photograph by Jeffrey W. Rubin.*

INTIMATE PROTEST
Jeff

At Home: Izanete Colla

Izanete Colla explained her role in the women's movement on a winter's day with her husband, Fernando Colla, and friend Ivone beside her near the *fogão* (cast-iron stove), which provided the three-room farmhouse's only source of heat. Impervious to the season, Izanete wore flip-flops, and her two kids were tumbling about on the floor and cuddling with her and Fernando while she spoke.

As a member of a Catholic Church commission in her town, Izanete witnessed the reality of women's place in society. They were there to do the laundry, from dishrags to religious garments. "Women were close to the domestic work, *always*," she said. "But at the moment when decisions were made, it was not the women who decided. It was at that moment that you sensed the difference."

For Izanete, the desire to be a part of the decision making had its roots in a new way of thinking about the land, which had at first seemed to be a dead end. As a teenager in the early 1980s, she knew intimately the discrimination her mother faced as a single mom in the countryside and the suffering her aunts experienced in their marriages, as well as the consequences of government policies that favored corporate agriculture over small farming. Rejecting this life, Izanete fled to the nearest town to finish high school, but her work as a maid did not pay enough to support her schooling and left her little time to study. After two years of working full time, without attending school at all, she met her husband, Fernando, who wanted to farm. Together they returned to the land.

It was an auspicious time for new ideas. A local NGO, the Center for Alternative Technologies, known as CETAP (Centro de Tecnologias Alternativas Populares), ran outreach and educational programs for farmers who wanted to adopt the new methods of organic and sustainable agriculture that were beginning to gain acceptance in the region. The NGO taught that there were ample resources at hand. It was from this sense of richness—not of poverty or need—that Izanete was moved: "I began to imagine, my God, our water is pure. And from there, the idea started: how to treat animals in a

Izanete Colla. *Photograph by Jeffrey W. Rubin.*

different way. And we began to cultivate the idea." Initially, their innovation was met with setbacks. A drought made starting up difficult, and the arrivals of two children increased their needs dramatically. Progress seemed again out of reach. "We didn't know how to change our history," she explained, recalling her efforts to create a new chapter of the Farmwomen associations in the tiny community where she lived. But the women couldn't commute easily among their far-flung homes, and Izanete herself didn't manage to get to the meetings. As her children grew, however, Izanete continued to search for a way to connect to like-minded women. She joined the Workers' Party in Ibiaçá, a small town nearby, and found her way to the women's movement there. The movement was a *luz acesa* (ray of light) for her: "I think that what stimulated me to stay here and to have hope of better days was the movement. I owe this to the movement. My life changed."

Izanete is a small, striking woman, with delicate bone structure and thin arms and hands. She gestures nonstop as she speaks. "It was an incredible difference," she recalled. At the women's movement meetings, she said, "You feel like you can do something." The contrast to the Church commission was immediate and indelible for her, and she took on the work of visiting her neighbors to persuade them to come to meetings, introducing them to the women's movement and its ideas. But it was no easy task to transmit her discovery to her peers. Standing in doorways and in kitchens, she heard again and again about male authority and a male God. At one women's movement meeting, the organizers led a *mística* of music and ritual to set the mood and encourage women to leave the constraints of home behind. They asked the participants if they felt themselves to be free. Izanete recalled the shocking response of one woman: "She answered, with complete frankness, that she thought that women are possessions of men, that she herself was a possession."

The role of the Christian God—traditionally, and utterly, male—casts a heavy shadow on the efforts of the women's movement. Izanete's own sister converted to evangelicalism, and Izanete has little patience for the newly strict practices her sister observed: "They brainwashed her!" she announced. Her sister had no time or money for the women's movement anymore, Izanete explained, or for talks on health care or the environment, or even for family celebrations. She had time only for her church and pastor. Izanete listed the things her sister and brother-in-law would no longer do: tell jokes, play games, drink wine. "She can't even wear shorts in the summer," she told us, appalled.

At this point Ivone recounted her own experience of facing resistance fueled by religion. When evangelicals tell her that women can't wear pants according to the Bible, she says to them, "You show me in what chapter or verse it says that pants are clothes for men." This does not encourage further conversation. She went on, "Because people know I think that way, because I won't say what I don't believe, right at that moment, people distance themselves from me. And that destroys a bit of the work I do." Ivone senses that for the women with whom she talks, "God functions as a way to explain yourself to yourself and know what you're feeling." She worried that the women she reached out to might fear that she was trying to take this sense of identity away from them. Seeing this, Ivone tries to suggest that what is perceived as fate, or destiny, may more appropriately be understood as politics. "I explain this relationship between politics and people's day-to-day lives," she said. "In reality, what makes things happen the way they do is politics." Izanete agreed. "The women don't see that they have credit and retirement benefits because the women's movement fought for them," she said. "The price of [farmers'] milk is terrible, so we protest. But we don't protest because we like to protest. We protest because there are people keeping the price of milk low."

However, problems that are not understood as political will not be fought with political means. Izanete described a popular radio program in which a psychologist tells listeners that "everything has to be flowers. Everything is the way you make it, the way you approach things." And Izanete describes the lengths to which women will go to improve their grounding in the family and the community. "They adore their role," she said. "When the nutritionist comes, they practically kneel at her feet, hoping to learn to cook even better for their husbands." The government has long played on this desire, sponsoring Mothers' Clubs, which since the 1980s have aimed to bring practical tools and a sense of belonging to rural women. Many of the members of these Mothers' Clubs are on Izanete's visiting list. She too is a mother, after all. But these women, she explained, "do whatever they can to keep the women's movement far away. For them, it's just cook, wash, iron, and cook." Women who attend Mothers' Club meetings return home the same as they left, she said, whereas the women's movement is about changing, about letting yourself be changed.

Sometimes Izanete does make headway with these women, and when she does, it is by building on the identity they value while encouraging new modes of practice. For example, she has succeeded at times in getting women—particularly mothers concerned about their young children's health—to question the use of genetically modified crops, which are infiltrating the region's agriculture. Such concerns echo her own conversion after she first began farming with her husband, but the women she works with often encounter trouble with their new ideas once they return home and find they can't convince their husbands to oppose the genetically modified seeds. When this happens, they are lost: "They distance themselves from the women's movement," Izanete explained, "so as not to feel this contradiction between what they know to be true and their husband's decisions in the home."

Genetically modified crops are the tip of the iceberg when it comes to such resistance. For the men, it seems, resistance to change is even more critical than it is for the women. "There are things that women can't manage to change in their husbands' heads," Izanete continued. Their husbands won't talk about sexually transmitted diseases, and they won't use condoms: "If the women try to insist on this, the men won't accept it. They can talk about it, but they can't manage to change things in practice."

Which raises the question of what role Fernando, sitting beside his wife on the kitchen bench, has played in her political awakening and increased dedication. Many women derive great pleasure from serving their husbands in traditional roles. Fernando, however, didn't want to be waited on hand and foot the way his father was, though he can't say when his way of thinking changed or even if it was a change. He asked, "How do I eat knowing there's a person serving me, who is living to please me, to make sure that everything is just right? I wouldn't be happy that way." In his choices, Fernando creates a space in which Izanete can be more fully human and have her own desires. This suggests that while the driver of women's progress in Brazil has undoubtedly been women organizing, protesting, dreaming, and canvassing, a critical ingredient for widespread uptake of the change is the willingness for both husband and wife to imagine a new way of being. Izanete captures the key contribution of activism when she recalls her first encounter with the women's movement, which gave her what the historian Rienhart Koselleck calls "a concept of historical hope."[1] "I feel important in the movement," she said, watching her children run playfully through the room. "Eu me sinto gente." It's a phrase difficult to translate without explanation, but perhaps none is required. It means, literally, "I feel like a person."

Izanete wants women to keep coming to movement meetings, but she knows there's no direct path to a different future. "Sometimes there are women who come," she observed, "and begin to change, but then they stop, they don't change any more." Looking back, it was from Izanete that I learned about this knot at the center of the women's movement. Leaders of the MMTR felt certain that they were fighting in the interests of all women. But then, why was it so hard to get more members, to continue the transformation that had begun so auspiciously with the marches and protests and trips to Brasília? Why was it so damned hard to change gender roles at home, to get men to do the dishes, to get men to take responsibility for doing the dishes, to get men to take responsibility for the health of the land and for their families' health, to talk about sex, to share in decision making, to caress and call their wives by name? Izanete couldn't answer these questions, but she readily acknowledged them.

After talking to Izanete, the confusing mix of messages at the women's movement meetings and the image of Mônica at the sink saying men should help with the dishes, as her husband smiled and put his feet up on the table, made more sense. I saw them through Izanete's eyes, as she showed me, piece by piece, what she was up against: the Catholic Church, pleasure in cooking, husbands who won't question genetically modified crops or wear condoms, the psychologist on the radio telling you that everything is flowers.

When I hear Izanete speak about Mothers' Clubs, Fernando ask how a man can eat while being served, and Ivone bypass religion for politics, I wonder first if they can't make the imaginative leap to understand what attracts people to these other worldviews. Yet what is most striking about our discussions, when I think about them a bit longer, is how genuinely aware and puzzled these three people are by the local world in which they live and which they seek to change: how much there is that works against them and confuses and complicates what they see to be true. "We know the world, and we read the world," Izanete told me, talking about the work of the alternative pharmacy in Ibiaçá, "and things go on from there."

In the Women's Pharmacy

The women's pharmacy in Ibiraiaras started from nothing in Odete Toazza's kitchen in the years after the women's movement won its big campaigns for legal and economic rights. Activists in the movement began talking more about health and sexuality and wanted "something concrete that they could do" in their communities. As the idea caught on, the MMTR got funds for equipment from German foundations and later from the governor, Olivio Dutra, a long-time supporter of the rural social movements. When Emma and I interviewed Odete, she wore her apron, covered her black curls with a hair net, and walked us through the complete preparation of an herbal remedy, explaining each step as she recounted her efforts to raise her children free of gender stereotypes despite her mother-in-law's fierce opposition. "It's not simply about mixing herbs," Odete told us. "It's about women having a good time. It's about women attacking the question of discrimination by meeting and forming groups, taking advantage of something concrete like the herbs to make a road to freedom for women." Odete and other women she knew in

Ibiraiaras looked to knowledge from the past and from advisors like Rafinha to make remedies from local plants. The syrups and salves they learned to produce promised relief for a wide range of illnesses, from stress and backaches to depression, high blood pressure, skin lesions, and cancer. The women also made scented soaps, skin lotions, and herbal teas with special capacities for healing typed out and pasted on the front of each bottle and package.

The first time I visited Ibiraiaras, in 2001, Gessi arranged for me to meet with the women who ran the pharmacy, now housed in the back kitchen of the farmers' union headquarters. I had already talked to the men who ran the union about the surge of activism inspired by the Catholic Church that had radicalized the unions and spawned the social movements of the southern countryside. Now the very women who had blocked highways and taken over buildings in these movements—and started their own—were cleaning and redesigning the kitchen in the union hall to house the women's pharmacy. To get there, I walked through the union reception area and the meeting room piled high with sacks of grain, out into the back hallway, and around the corner to a door splayed with feminist logos and posters of pregnant women and natural seeds. Then I walked through the door to the kitchen, with its big central table. There the group of six women who collectively ran the pharmacy showed me how they dried and prepared the plants they used for remedies, storing them in carefully marked dark-brown jars on shelves along the wall. Before we sat down to talk, they explained what additional ingredients they needed to complete their inventory, how long each dried plant and liquid would last, and how and at what temperatures they combined them. The women contrasted their own medicines with the pharmaceutical products widely marketed for depression and other illnesses in rural Brazil, suggesting that the commercial medicines resembled the fertilizers that had transformed agriculture and poisoned their environment since the 1970s, when the banks and large landholders began to take the lead in agricultural production.

My questions about gender brought quick responses. In the animated discussion, I did not think to ask each woman to identify herself before she spoke, so in many cases I'm not sure who said what. "What we try to put into women's heads," one of the participants began, "is that they were not made to enslave themselves to men, that we have equal rights, and we have to achieve them." This had its corollary for men, too: "They weren't made to be workhorses, to do nothing but work on the farm, but also to be partners." So the

MMTR focused on changing the domination of men over women into dialogue between them. "We're all in the movements, fighting for a decent life," another woman emphasized. "We're also in the movements as families, families that work together, educating our children." Even as they sought to identify and deepen what they saw as women's skills and affinities, such as nurturing and healing, the women in the pharmacy insisted that the work of men and women shouldn't be different. Women have always done farmwork, so men should start to do housework. "But the men get a complex about it, and they say, 'I'm doing women's work.'"

Inés Marchesini talked about how her son is changing. "Before, when other women or girls would come to the house, he'd stop doing housework because he was ashamed. Today, no. He's more aware now. And now my husband also clears the table, and if people come over, he doesn't stop doing it, not for a second, he continues." Changes within the family thus need to be public as well, and they have to occur across the board. "We have to make our sons realize," Inés went on, "that they have to do everything, because we don't have this thing about men's work and women's work anymore." Kids get other messages in school, however. When Elena's son was in second grade his teacher corrected him when he answered her question, "Who is the head of the household?" He came home in tears. "I told the teacher that in our house it's not like that," the boy told Elena, "that we live together and we don't have a *chefe* or *chefa* [a male or female head of household]. We're equal, we all decide things together. But the teacher said that there has to be a head, and it's the father."

On the path to equality and dialogue in families, taking on new tasks isn't easy. When women brought home the first pamphlets about sexuality that the MMTR produced, they didn't have the courage to talk about them with friends or family members, so they hid the booklets in their dresser drawers.[2] Then, through conversations with feminist advisors from Porto Alegre who had experience talking openly about sex, the local women began learning to speak without embarrassment. "So now when it's time to talk to our children," one of them explained, "it's not so difficult. It's clear that education and our group conversations were basic for this. Suddenly things that you wouldn't even tell to your doctor, here in our groups we laugh about them, so that by speaking we open up a lot of things."

It's difficult to bring what have been private fears and shames into public view, even when these experiences are replicated in so many households.

Generally, one of the women observed with sadness, when lots of farmwomen get together at a women's movement meeting, "they say, 'it hurts, it hurts here, it hurts there.' These pains show us another reality; they tell us something." Sitting around the table in the kitchen in the union hall, their voices lilting and interweaving while men conducted union business outside, the women focused squarely on the power and intransigence of the men with whom they live. "So many women talk about the violence in their houses, from husbands and from sons," one explained. Another began her comment with the official cadences of the women's movement and ended it right in the middle of daily life: "We, the women of the countryside of Rio Grande do Sul, we were very oppressed, because the head of the household is always the man, and this vision is really strong, even today. So we try to explain and educate at home, that everyone has to participate, to divide the responsibilities. But it's still all around, this idea that the place of women is by the sink and the stove." And from this place where they stand, or are expected to stand, they see a path to a different future: "I think that the movement was a road for all of us here. I mean for me it was, a road to living in a different way, not the way society imposes. And we know that we have to live fully, with our emotions, we have to embrace our mates without malice, the embrace of a partner."

If the women's movement opens up a new space of expectation, participating in the movement brings its own pain. As one member of the pharmacy team pointed out, "Some women joke that it was easier when they weren't in the movement, because they didn't get involved in these things. Now I get involved, I want to change things, and I'm filled with anguish." In this situation, day-to-day life becomes a place of old and new together, as women approach daily tasks and relationships with new demands. "I don't accept it when things happen in the old ways, and I end up suffering with this. It creates conflict and tension," another woman added. But whatever the cost, she said, she was committed to the future that she and her colleagues imagine: "I have a love for all this. I can't turn myself off, no matter how hard it is."

In the pharmacy, I was struck by the women's concreteness, how every abstract issue they talked about played out in daily life, and every cultural or emotional force occurred, in their telling, in a world of economics. In Rio Grande do Sul, the pharmacy women told me, wives are involved in production, but not commercialization. Women don't go to markets with the vegetables they produce, because they have to do the housework and cleaning. Even when men stay home, the men don't do housework. But these clearly defined roles no longer mean tranquil families, one farmwoman explained: "Because if the woman participates in production, and at the moment of business she doesn't go because the housework wouldn't get done otherwise, for me that's a problem. It's everyone's responsibility to deal with money. It's good for the man, but it's also good for the woman."

At the end of our conversation in the pharmacy, the women talked about the difficulty and necessity of accepting disorder at home. At meetings, I had heard many lectures about the need for women to do less housework and take some time for rest or conversation: to prepare one main dish instead of three, to stop ironing socks and underwear, to leave the front porch unswept. Each of the women in the pharmacy claimed to like everything in its place, cleaned and polished, but they had different strategies for cutting themselves slack.

"Virgin Maria," one of the women exclaimed, "I like to clean, but you won't find everything in my house shining." "Organizing is one thing," another agreed, "but cleaning all day is another."

"In my house," Elena explained, "it's the opposite. In my mess I find things. If I put everything in order, I wouldn't participate in the movement, I wouldn't drink my chimarão, I wouldn't have time for my partner, it wouldn't work."

The others found that amusing. "Elena couldn't find her raffle booklet," Gessi recounted laughing, "and it turned out it was stuck in the Bible."

How do they manage to do everything? "I need half the day to make lunch." "I have to plan out lunch the night before." "You have to rest." "You do what you can." "What's missing is the night for sleeping." "The most difficult thing," one of the women concluded, "is the part that's in our blood that says making bread is a woman's job. You have to do it and leave everything shining, because if you don't, God forgive you if your neighbor arrives and finds your house a mess."

That's what the women fight so hard to change when they bring the women's movement home, and they are slowly gaining ground. "My husband and son-in-law watched me," one of the pharmacy women reported. "They watched how I did things, and now they do them. Before, they didn't clear the table, they didn't do anything. But now, I get home and everything is arranged. And not because I insisted. They learned because they wanted to."

In the pharmacies, women learn because they want to, and they learn about health and marketing, as well as gender. Perhaps that's why the pharmacies appeal to all factions within the women's movement, from Vera and Gessi, who join unions and municipal governments, to Salete and Adriana, who insist that the women's movement must ally with more hierarchical and male-led movements in the streets to challenge the government. All of them find value in these new, small, often makeshift local initiatives that bring women right back to the stove and conversation.

Within a month of my visit to the Ibiraiaras pharmacy in 2001, the women there, like small groups of women throughout the state, received new stoves, refrigerators, and tables through a pharmacy grant that the MMTR secured from the state government. Within six months, they attended a series of three-day workshops with more than thirty other women from towns throughout the Ronda Alta region. At the workshops thick, bubbling syrups were produced from scratch and issues from transnational agriculture to intimate marital relations were held up for examination. Within two years, the Ibiraiaras women outfitted an adjoining room for massage; within four they sent one of their own members for professional massage training and put a heater in the massage room for cold winter afternoons, an unheard of luxury among poor farmers; and five years after our conversation they were running a store, Quitanda, in the center of town. Quitanda, located just across from the church and the Esso gas station, sells local organic produce; handicrafts; foods such as bread, preserved fruit, and brown sugar; and rows upon rows of the women's salves and lotions, all neatly labeled. At the end of a visit to Ibiraiaras in 2008, I stopped in to say goodbye to Mônica, who worked as one of the store's coordinators. Quitanda had become a hub of local activity. Farmwomen in town for doctors' appointments or errands stopped in to catch up on recent news, buy medicine or groceries, or find a ride home. Taxi drivers from the stand across the street dropped in for snacks or to pick up fares. Mônica worked the cash register and took messages, coordinating the comings and goings of local friends and acquaintances.

As I embraced Mônica to say goodbye once more, I looked straight through Quitanda's enormous front window, spotless and sparkling in the bright winter sun. I noted what the women saw from their store: the downtown street with its trucks and taxis and passersby, the flowering gardens of the town plaza, the enormous round church, the newly refurbished hospital, and the rows of houses on cobblestone streets beyond. The pharmacy women had made it to the center of town, and they looked straight out over everything.

In the Union: Vera Fracasso

When she was growing up, Vera Fracasso admired the way her father worked to end corruption in the union and make it a real force for defending farmers. Thinking back to the origins of her activism, she remembered how he also controlled everything at home, which "didn't sit well in the head of a young person." Vera did not set out to be a revolutionary, and she never accepted the path to deeper radicalism that attracted some of the MMTR's other founders, who rejected participation in existing political institutions. But she stuck to her guns on gender, and refused to let the complete submission and silencing of the women around her continue. Vera's path in life proceeded from that focused determination, and eventually her world was entirely different from her mother's. She had indeed transformed what it meant to be a woman in her family and community. She became president of the local farmers' union, married someone who respects her work, and raised her sons to question conventional gender roles.

Vera got involved in activism, she said, *por gosto* for the pleasure of it, when the priests and nuns came to her parents and asked them to allow their daughter to join a Church youth group. Vera remembers meeting Gessi and the other women from Ibiraiaras, Sananduva, Passo Fundo, and farther away, women who came of age together, founded the MMTR, and attended each other's weddings and the baptisms of their children. She recounts her close relationship with Sister Valesca, with whom she traveled from town to town. Together they stayed overnight in the houses of farmwomen who gave them food and encouragement as they began conversations about women's rights.

Vera thinks hard about gender issues and what it is she hopes can be different in the future. She's not sure. Vera is simultaneously daring in her rejection of her mother's worldview and cautious in what she thinks might come next. Late one night, after Vera had spent the day canvassing farm families and the evening studying for her university classes, we talked at length in the union hall in Sananduva. She wore wire-rimmed glasses, and straight, chin-length black hair framed her narrow face. When our conversation shifted from Vera's role in the MMTR to her beliefs about gender, she asked me how it had come about that I studied a women's movement and cared so much about gender issues. I told her about my coming-of-age in the late sixties and early seventies in the United States, when the women's movement was flourishing, and the commitment born then—and strained but not abandoned since—

Vera Fracasso. *Photograph by Jeffrey W. Rubin.*

that men and women could occupy the same roles and even have the same emotions and sensibilities in a society or a marriage. "But that's not what we mean here," Vera answered briskly. "We're not talking about being the same. We're talking about mutual respect."

I've tried to press Vera on what she means by mutual respect and what she thinks regarding how her sons will grow up, what kind of men they will become. In Sananduva as in the United States, few people have imagined what truly open choices might produce. Vera is clear that she believes each person should decide for himself or herself about what to do in the world. But what is the range of choices? In a conversation in her garden, Vera told Emma and me that men will value women's activities more when they see the economic benefits of those activities. As she thought out loud, she wavered between the notion of distinct, complementary roles for men and women and the idea that real choice might lead to no fixed roles at all. "Differences were greater in the past," Vera noted. "People should choose their tasks." But she recognizes the demands of survival in a developing country like Brazil. "Tasks have to be divided up," she admits, "but that doesn't signify submission for either one."

Could she imagine a future of men with the same capacities and roles as women? Vera says she could, but it will take a long time to get there—because women want to keep the power that they have. "In my family, I've managed to innovate and get beyond that. My sons will deal with it even better. The role that I do automatically as a woman, my sons will find it normal to do for themselves." But, Vera went on, "I see the contradictions of this in my house. I have three men who are under my power. It's a big dilemma, how to use that power. And when we get together, we women, we talk about these questions. We like this power. It's something that at times appears tyrannical. But we, who according to society don't command anything, and are always submissive. . . . Well, let's see, we do command."

Vera's chosen task is to turn the private, indirect power that women wield in families into public power, exercised in a democratic fashion. To create a space for herself among male union leaders, Vera had to learn to speak in new ways: "You have to say no, my way of doing things is different." Vera talks about understanding herself as a woman and holding on to that part of herself. Forging a place when people aren't ready to receive her brings a mix of hardship and great satisfaction. Vera appears comfortable where she is now, convinced that the farmers' union is better because women have joined it. But she knows not everyone agrees with her. "It's cool to have a woman as one of a group of union leaders. What's not cool is for a woman to be president." Vera says that she can lead a male union with a woman's voice, just as she explains that women can balance work and family without undue difficulty. As she speaks, though, with her eyes looking more at the ground than at us, it is clear that these have been hard-won achievements. Vera tells of being passed over for the union presidency once and letting it go. The second time, she insisted on running and won the position. "I said, okay, guys, now you can't say that I'm a woman and I can't do it."

Vera broke with the headquarters of the women's movement in 1997, when it began directly to support the MST and the breakaway union for small farmers that the MST endorsed, the Movement of Small Farmers, known as MPA (Movimento de Pequenos Agricultores). It wasn't that Vera couldn't accept the MST's radical stance, though she disagreed with it fundamentally. Rather, Vera couldn't accept that women in the women's movement should have to adopt one single view and fall into line behind a majority position. Vera wanted dialogue and space for different visions within the women's movement—what I'd call pluralism. When she left the MMTR, Vera didn't see herself as leaving the women's movement entirely; as Gessi did years later, she continued to see herself as a women's movement activist and to organize events in her town. Vera left the formal movement and ceased to be part of the executive committee and attend leadership meetings, not because she was thrown out, and not because the other leaders of the MMTR weren't elected or she couldn't have run an opposition campaign (though she doubts she could have won). Vera left the MMTR leadership because she couldn't stand to be there.

Vera felt mistreated and marginalized, outmaneuvered by a political rough-and-tumble that contradicted everything she believed in about collective action and consensus. Vera had no schooling in the harshness of democratic politics. She had been trained for activism by the radical church, with visions of social justice and of organizing and mobilizing for rights against entrenched structures of power. The Catholic Church told women to look for consensus. Vera had no experience with the argumentative kind of dialogue that Rafinha and Elsi, at the workshop in Santa Lucia, had counseled women to learn, despite their discomfort.

"I don't know why I left, why I didn't fight back," Vera told me in the union hall. "I didn't see what was coming, and I didn't know how to make the right arguments. So I opted to leave." But despite her success in leading the farmers' union, Vera saw how much women needed the space of a women's movement.

"So what will we do?" she wondered. "We are the MMTR, so why do we have to create another women's movement? Why isn't this one ours?" Two years later, having experienced more of the successes of leading the union and the costs of no longer being part of a movement, Vera went further: "I should have fought back. Other women would have supported me. The movement is ours too."

Vera knows that political power, like women's power in their families, has to be understood and handled with care. In her personal life, she refused her mother's submissiveness and her father's linking of domination at home to progressive politics outside. Still, she stayed in her hometown, with a husband who respected her political work, and brought up their sons with a new openness about gender roles. In politics, Vera rejected institutions that did not welcome individual voices and democratic decision making. She opposes the MST because of its radical approach to political change, and because decisions are made by leaders and then handed down to everyone else.

"What is power, and how do you exercise it?" Vera wonders. In her view, the leaders of movements that are run from the center want to divide up power and use it as their own, to command others. But she wants to be a steward of power: "I can't be in the same place forever. Other people are going to come to take my place. And power too, it has to be understood as a space to speak and grow for a whole movement, not for me as an individual."

Vera's conclusion about power was also about what the MMTR might have been, what democratic politics in Brazil might have been and might yet be. Vera left the MMTR because she believed democracy had left it, that a few women at the top were making the important decisions and subordinating the women's movement to the goals of the larger and more powerful MST. Perhaps a hard-fought campaign over the long haul could have kept the women's movement democratic. Vera left and didn't look back, except with her deep nostalgia for the movement as inspiration and guide. "We women need a source for clear thinking, and for us the movement was that source," she explained. "And today we don't have that anymore." Without the movement in her life, Vera observed, she finds herself taking missteps or compromising when she should stand firm. "Because the questions in our lives are so profound that you need constantly to be analyzing and rethinking them, or in an instant you find yourself doing things that just a short while ago you wouldn't have done."

As I worked for years to solve the puzzle of the MMTR, why it had shifted so dramatically over time and why women like Vera, Elenice, and Gessi had left, I came to see what a movement in democracy might be and how the MMTR come so close to being that. I saw the leaders who had left, the priests and advisors who watched, the women who joined the invasion of Aracruz Inc., and the women who ran events in their towns. I saw all of them reach for a language to describe a new kind of movement, in the streets and in the institutions, autonomous and flexible, tolerant of disagreement. That's part of what a movement is, envisioning a future whose outlines you just begin to see.

"It's about being happy," Vera told me. She rejects that part of the Catholic Church that ignores happiness, just as she rejects the MST for its suppression of dissent and the broader silencing this promotes: "What good does it do to fight for a more just society if I don't . . . grow, feel valorized, feel good, if I can't have my family, my sons, my husband, my community. If I were sad." To want a just society, Vera told me, "doesn't mean to give up the right to be happy in the process." Or the right to your own voice.

DEMANDING SPEECH
AND ENDURING SILENCE

Emma

Ivone and Vania met leading women's movement protests, taking over government buildings to secure legal rights and insisting on women's autonomy on public streets and in private homes. In 1994 they moved in together, making an alternative vision a reality in their own lives. Seven years later, they moved to a red-and-white house in Ibiraiaras, and Gessi and Didi built their own house in Ivone and Vania's front yard.

Gessi and Didi's daughter, Natália, who was three when I first met her and thirteen when I last visited, runs back and forth between the two houses to collect ingredients for shared meals, and her brother, Davi, is as comfortable in his aunts' house as in his own. This alternative household arrangement—more typical of Northampton, Massachusetts, where I grew up, than a Catholic town in Southern Brazil—is built on two decades of courage and audacity. It comes out of a generation of young female leaders who refused to settle for limited lives and instead started a women's movement, showing the world and showing themselves the possibility of new possibilities. And it rests on two lesbian women who have learned to trade the right to speak about themselves for the right to live as they choose.

Ivone, Vania, and other movement leaders insisted that to engage rural women in a project to change the world, each woman needed to see herself as a citizen with rights, and she needed a place to speak about herself. They worked to facilitate open conversations in rural homes and at movement meetings. The first time I saw Vania, she was standing in a church basement in jeans and a women's movement T-shirt, surrounded by a circle of women and leading everyone in song. When she paused, her face took shape around her wide smile, short-cropped brown hair jutting out across her forehead. I was twelve years old, visiting a women's movement gathering with my family, and it was clear right away that I had stumbled into a place from which real change was being made. As night fell and the flow of trucks on the dirt road outside the church in Santa Lucia slowed, I watched the women prepare a communal meal and then throw squares of paper inscribed with hopes for their families into a bowl of fire.

Vania Zamboni and Ivone Bonês. *Photograph by Jeffrey W. Rubin.*

The stories I heard when Dad and I returned to Ibiraiaras three years later got beyond what the movement achieved and showed me what it took to get there, painting a picture not only of what the movement is now, but also of what it might have become. Over the years, I came to know a quieter but equally dedicated side of Ivone and Vania, a side their neighbors in Ibiraiaras and their comrades in the movement refused to take on.

I asked Ivone and Vania if they would talk to me about their relationship not knowing how they would respond. Though Porto Alegre has one of the most active gay rights movements in the world, the urban movement has yet to extend to rural areas. To the contrary, Catholic influence in rural areas like Ibiraiaras is such that when the women's movement began discussing sex and birth control in the early 1990s, the Church, which was instrumental in encouraging young activists to form an autonomous women's movement in the 1980s, temporarily stopped letting the women's movement use church spaces for meetings. Ivone's and Vania's names were almost always mentioned in the same sentence—"Ivone and Vania will be here soon," or, to Gessi's children, "go ask your aunts if you can stay at their house tonight"—but I would never have known they were partners, and not sisters or friends, if my family hadn't stayed in their house on my first trip to Ibiraiaras in 2002. They were never physically affectionate in public, and in the months I have spent at women's movement meetings, community barbecues, and Gessi's kitchen table with the two families, I have never heard Ivone and Vania's relationship mentioned in any explicit way.

There is one story—a success story—I could have told without ever talking to Ivone and Vania about their relationship. In a deeply patriarchal and religious part of Brazil, the nation with the world's largest Roman Catholic population, two women live together in a red-and-white house in the center of town and have never been hurt or forced to move.

There's also a more nuanced story, which is the story Ivone and Vania chose to tell me. It's a story of two women who each day live the paradox of exclusion in the face of tolerance and silence in a space of speech.

I didn't know at first if talking about homosexuality was taboo in Ibiraiaras, or if Ivone and Vania's relationship was so obvious as to make speech unnecessary. I got my answer at lunch one day in Gessi's house, where the two families almost always ate, when my dad mentioned that gay marriage had been legalized in our state of Massachusetts. For the first time I can remember, the table of eight fell silent. Didi leaned his chair back. Gessi changed the subject. Everyone resumed talking, and I wondered what was so unspeakable about the relationship of the two women seated next to me.

A few days later, Ivone and Vania asked my dad and me to have dinner at their house, and they picked up the conversation that had fallen flat in Gessi's kitchen. Their kitchen is smaller than Gessi's, but there was plenty of room for the four of us. Ivone squeezed orange juice while Dad and I set the table and Vania poured homemade wine from two-liter soda bottles as always, the two women dressed similarly in women's movement T-shirts and jeans.

I visited Ibiraiaras in 2002, 2004, 2007, 2008, and 2012. Some of my strongest memories from my time there are the dinners in Ivone and Vania's small kitchen, a table that was predictably set and a conversation that was always honest and always changing. After the initial dinner with my father, I began to go back alone, finding that when it was just the three of us, a guard came down that I hadn't noticed when he was there. My conversations with Ivone and Vania shaped the curriculum I ultimately designed, which moved beyond celebrating the movement's achievements to explore the challenges of activism, and the conversations shaped me. I learned from Ivone and Vania that it's never perfectly clear when to stay silent and when to speak, but that it matters what we choose to speak about and what sides of other people, and what sides of ourselves, we choose to silence or push away. I learned that speaking can be uncertain and painful, but that silence sometimes comes at a greater cost.

Ivone and Vania first met traveling to rural communities throughout the state, knocking on doors, sipping chimarão, and persuading women to join the movement. "We traveled around together," Vania explained. "In the first community, Ivone and I stayed in the same house. We had to share a bed, that night and the next one. In the next community we stayed in different houses. That afternoon Ivone brought everyone . . ."

"No, you came over to my house." Ivone was a stickler for details, always ready with the exact dates and locations to fill in a story no one had ever asked about or been willing to hear. But Vania wasn't one to back down.

"No, the other way around."

"Remember? In the afternoon you came with . . ."

"Ivone came with some of the people she was with over to the house I was in. We sat in a circle talking and she was next to me. I remember she put her arm on my knee." Vania bent her elbow and rested it on her knee. "Just like that. It was nothing and yet it was significant. . . . The next night we were at the same house. She was in bed and I kind of jumped in," Vania lurched forward in her chair, "and Ivone laughed and said, 'Vania!' I wondered why a man and a woman can hug each other but two women can't."

"I think the relationship we created doesn't have an explanation," she said. "You can't say how it started, why it started. . . . Why does this happen, that two women like each other, that two women live together? There's psychology to explain some things, but the value of our relationship is the way we live and what happens between us."

Ivone lifted her hand from her chin. Her hands moved as she spoke, from her heart outward and then above her head, flying along with her words. When the relationship began, people told her, "It won't work out. Where are you going to live together? You won't survive. Society won't permit you to live that way."

Ivone and Vania defied their fathers and started a women's movement while still in their teens. They traveled on buses to the capital of Brazil to protest in front of government buildings. When government officials wouldn't talk to them, they took over capitol buildings, demanding rights for women in a notoriously religious and patriarchal country. They were not about to limit their lives to what society would permit.

Ivone traces the courage that allowed them to move in together to their experience in the women's movement. "We always said that for us, the movement was an alternative way of being, a way to change our lives, to change how we behave, to free ourselves. . . . So why couldn't we create something different, why couldn't we create a different life for ourselves?" Crafting an alternative lifestyle with Vania, Ivone added, and seeing that such a life was possible, kept her committed to the women's movement even as many colleagues chose other paths.

But the open and equal world the movement envisioned—the world in which women could explore alternative visions and speak about themselves—remained closed to the two women who helped create it. Ivone and Vania shared a mattress the night the movement took over a government building and refused to leave until the governor agreed to negotiate with them, and the time the bus died on the way back from a mobilization in Brasilia and women tumbled out to sleep on the side of the road. Yet there was no space for them to speak about the central relationship in their lives, and any time they tried to bring up homosexuality in the women's movement—in the very space that claimed to welcome women's experiences—Ivone and Vania were met with silence.

That silence silenced them. For years, Ivone and Vania suggested homosexuality as a topic for the movement newsletter, which was distributed to movement participants. Women were encouraged to submit topics, but Ivone and Vania's suggestion never appeared. Vania said, "It felt like hiding, the way I didn't say anything and people didn't have the courage to ask." Sometimes she tried to bring up the relationship with her family, with Gessi and two of Ivone's other sisters, and later with her own nephew, who Vania says was the only one in either family to broach the subject himself. No one was angry or cold, Vania explained, "But it stopped there. A month, two months . . . it didn't go on. I was going to have to insist again. But then I didn't feel the desire to speak." In the movement, speech about the relationship was cut off from the beginning. In Ivone's and Vania's families, when spaces of speech opened, they quickly shut down.[1]

Ivone and Vania had spoken about their relationship so rarely that sometimes it seemed as if they were telling each other their sides of the story by sharing it

with me. After they described how they met, Vania said, "and so our relationship grew, with excitement and fear."

"Fear?" Ivone looked up sharply.

"Ivone. Fear, you know."

"Yes, it was hard sometimes in the beginning. But not anymore."

"It is hard, still," Vania broke in. "If something happens between Ivone and
me, there's no one to talk to."

Ivone shrugged. "I've always had something in me that makes me do what I
want. I've learned that it doesn't matter what other people think, that you have
to know what you are." She went on to say that she and Vania know to make
sure their curtains are always closed, that they would never hold hands in the
street, and I saw a more vulnerable side of this headstrong leader, this dedicated woman whose pain in the closed world forced upon her comes in part
from her efforts to open the world for so many others.

When it comes to fighting for the change she wants to see in the world,
Ivone's way has never been one of silence. In 1998, when policemen prevented
Ivone and other leaders of the women's movement from entering the governor's office building in Porto Alegre, she led a takeover of the building. More
than a thousand women stormed inside and refused to leave until the governor negotiated with them about women's health care. When three months
passed and no steps had been taken to make available the health services
to which women were legally entitled, Ivone returned to the capital. She
instructed women to enter the building inconspicuously in pairs, gather
in the bathroom, and then take over the hallways once again. Now, in her
kitchen, Ivone was telling me that in some parts of your life, you take what you
can get. When women don't have the right to maternity leave, you take over
government buildings. But when the women's movement you helped start
refuses to talk about homosexuality, you talk about other things. The conces-
sions become so familiar it's almost possible to forget that not everyone lives
this way, never able to say my boyfriend, my partner, my wife, the person
I love.

In the movement and in their town, Ivone and Vania learned firsthand the
pain that comes from silence, the shame that comes from living your daily life
knowing that who you are and how you live is unspeakable. They didn't want
to damage a movement that protected other women from this pain by demanding a space in the movement for themselves. Instead, Ivone and Vania
lived the paradox of silence amid speech, each day facing the limits of what

could be talked about even as they fought to make speech more possible and more meaningful for rural women across Brazil.

They faced the limits of speech until they couldn't face them anymore. In 2003, Ivone and Vania left the movement, amid disagreements with other leaders about the couple's work as paid movement organizers. Vania took a job as a truck driver, and Ivone began cleaning someone else's home. They still lead gatherings of women in their town, but they no longer hold leadership positions in the movement. "This is what I think about the story of our leaving the movement," Ivone told me when I asked. "It was the place where we worked and it was a place where there wasn't space for us. I think that it's a form of repression . . . that if the movement was what sustained you, the base from which you could speak, from which you could work, then you can't have a larger debate, you can't advance, if you don't have space there. So you have to do something."

When what you do—whether that's working in the institutions, going back to school, or moving in with another woman—isn't welcome, when the movement ceases to be the open space you've fought to create, it's hard to stay. Strong leaders brought their dedication elsewhere, or, like Ivone and Vania, left the movement not knowing where to direct their extraordinary enthusiasm and skill. These former movement leaders continue to fight for women's rights in union halls, government offices, university classrooms, and meetings of local women. What they lost was the possibility of continuing to collaborate, strengthening and making real their vision for women in Brazil, and the possibility of having for themselves the kind of open space they worked to create for others.

PART III

Moving Forward

10

"WHEN YOU SPEAK OF CHANGES"

Emma

Three days after my high school graduation, in 2007, Dad and I boarded a plane for Brazil. The trip felt familiar: Hartford to Atlanta, Atlanta to São Paulo, São Paulo to Porto Alegre. It was the same trip we had taken with my mom and sisters in 2001, when my family lived in Porto Alegre for a year, and in 2004, when Dad and I first did research on our own. As we drove the highways and dirt roads to Ibiraiaras in June of 2007, I realized that things felt both shakier and more secure this time. Dad and I had worked together for three years, teaching classes, running workshops, and writing profiles. A collaboration that felt kind of crazy when we first drove into Ibiraiaras had become an exciting part of our lives. But we knew that things wouldn't be quite the same this time. I was older and had more to say, the women's lives had surely changed, and we brought with us a curriculum we had taught about the women's movement in the United States and profiles we had written of Gessi, Ivone, and Vania, which we planned to show them.

As a twelve-year-old, I had watched these women plan demonstrations and lead others in song, and I pictured their younger selves starting a movement when they weren't much older than me. They hadn't waited for their parents' permission, or for some template or person to show them how to make a movement come alive. In many ways, they cleared the path as they created it, constantly dreaming up new ways of fighting for women's rights despite all that stood in their way.

I wanted to know how they did it, so as soon as my family returned from our year in Brazil, I started asking when we could go back. Dad, whose research fellowship had covered our expenses for the year, joked that I should come up with my own project. He didn't really mean it, but during my first year of high school, when I took him seriously and suggested that we do a project together, he listened—perhaps because he had heard Gessi's, Ivone's, and Vania's stories about fathers who didn't listen to them. Those stories shaped me too. Looking back, I think I dared to imagine making a curriculum about the women's movement because the women I met in Brazil showed me that it's okay to act on my ideas before there are models or people to show me the way. Their activism, in its varied forms, let me see a way to a new kind of project, and a

Ivone Bonês. *Photograph by Jeffrey W. Rubin.*

new kind of collaboration, that in a very small way let me join them in their gamble on change.

When Dad and I first decided to make a curriculum about the women's movement, we didn't know if it would work. Schools in the United States don't normally use examples of Brazilian social movements to teach students about citizenship and democracy. But my first lessons in what it means to be a citizen, to be aware of issues facing your community and engaged in addressing them, had come from Brazilian women who transformed their communities with fewer resources and less education than I had when we met. Dad and I liked the idea of teaching other students about a movement that had so moved us. So we bought a video camera and booked plane tickets, then spent a month interviewing leaders of the women's movement, attending movement meetings, and spending afternoons in women's homes.

The curriculum began to take shape my junior year of high school, when my principal agreed to let me teach a class to middle school students. I decided to teach about two other Brazilian social movements alongside the women's movement: the MST and Afro Reggae, a group that uses dance and drumming to keep kids off the streets in the poorest shantytowns of Rio de Janeiro. I taught the class as an elective. Week by week, watching my students' reactions and bouncing ideas off my dad, I put together a series of lesson plans. I used clips from interviews, played songs written by women's movement activists, and planned the kinds of debates, art projects, and role plays my favorite teachers had used in their classes.

My students read letters that Brazilian activists wrote to President Lula, then wrote letters of their own. Some wrote to President Bush, others to the mayor of their towns, and others to the principal of the school. They debated whether landless workers should be allowed to take over idle land, and, in a parallel fictional debate that brought the issue closer to home, whether Americans with third homes should be obligated to allow victims of Hurricane Katrina to move in. The names of women's movement activists—Gessi, Ivone, Vania, Mônica, Vera, and Elenice—became common terms in our classroom as students watched video clips of the women speaking and read early drafts of the profiles I later brought back to Ibiraiaras. When I raised the question of what we make of Mônica still doing the dishes, even as she says she shouldn't have to, one eighth grader jumped in with an explanation of why "it's not just talk," because "talk matters." He based his argument on something Ivone had said about the role of speech in making change and on his own experiences at home.

"I don't know if I would be that brave," a sixth grader said after hearing Gessi's story of facing dogs and grenades. Dad and I were teaching an afternoon workshop on the women's movement at the elementary school I had attended. In the video, Gessi remembers how "We started moving and the dogs and policemen started to walk backward, walk backward, and we kept walking forward." In the classroom in Northampton, Massachusetts, a young woman responded by asking herself, would I have done the same thing? Will I ever have to?

The year after I taught the class at my school, I tried turning it into a curriculum that other teachers could use. With Dad's input, I put together a binder of lesson plans, student worksheets, and a DVD. We then contacted Latin America centers at universities across the country, many of which agreed to sponsor day-long workshops for public school teachers and professors interested in brainstorming new ways of teaching about Latin America. We presented our curriculum in workshops at Yale, Harvard, Brown, Duke, and the University of California, San Diego (UCSD), and the strength of the teachers' responses gave the project momentum. They were excited at the possibility of using these lessons to supplement curricula that presented Latin America through a handful of facts spread across a textbook page, if at all, and to draw in Brazilian and other Latino students. Several teachers related the violence and depriva- tion in Brazilian shantytowns to the neighborhoods in which they taught. Others saw their own stories and those of their female students in the inter- views with women's movement activists like Mônica and Elenice.

Most teachers talked about how happy Mônica seemed, even as she worked from dawn until midnight milking the cows, preparing food for her family, and cleaning up after everyone had gone to sleep, because she spoke about her work with such confidence and pride. But one woman at a workshop in New Haven, a wiry, middle-aged guidance counselor who had been quiet until the discussion of Mônica, said, "That woman is *not* happy. That woman is op- pressed. I know women like Mônica." After reading an interview with Elenice Pastore, the former movement leader whose father forced her to quit school after eighth grade, a Latina teacher in San Diego said that she had won a full scholarship to UCSD, but her mother refused to let her go to college. "If you do that," her mother said, "no man will ever marry you." The teacher turned down the scholarship, and then, years later, had to pay her own way through college. She and other teachers in San Diego said the story wasn't outdated. The families of many of the girls in their classes continue to expect their daughters to take on traditional female roles and not venture far from home.

To suggest that American students have something in common with, and something to learn from, the efforts of women in Brazil is to go against the direction knowledge usually takes. Most schools in the United States focus on U.S. history; when they teach about other countries today, they often do so through the lens of foreign policy. When Dad and I suggest that issues facing a community in Brazil might not be so far from home for students here, we're taking a markedly different approach from traditional curricula and from American politicians, who speak of spreading democracy, not learning about it from people in other parts of the world.

We returned to Ibiraiaras in 2007 to share the curriculum with the women it featured, and to see what was happening in their lives. Gessi's job in the health department had ended in 2004, when the mayor who appointed her lost in the municipal elections. Gessi wasn't sure what to focus on next. Didi started working longer hours on the farm, and Gessi, Ivone, and Vania pieced to- gether whatever jobs they could find. Ivone had taken care of cooking and cleaning for both families when Gessi worked full time in the health department. Once Gessi was no longer employed, Ivone worked as maid for another family, and Gessi took over her sister's role. During one of the many afternoons I spent in Gessi's kitchen, she set me up cutting potatoes at the sink, then swept the floor, set the table, entertained her son, and deflected complaints from Didi, all without pause. But I could tell she was tired, and on a different day, when we were in the kitchen alone, Gessi told me that after running a health department, it was tough reimmersing herself in the daily work of her own family.

Didi's father died in 2006, and now Didi spent most of his time working on his father's land. His family was worried about him, and I was too, especially when he spoke about his sudden love of silence—he who had grabbed the microphone in moments of crisis—and of not knowing what to do next. He still attended city council meetings as an elected representative, but he spent a lot of time playing *bola*, a horseshoes-like game, with other men in a building at the edge of town. He was gruff at home, and he and Gessi argued more. Two decades after Didi defied his father to join the movements, financial concerns felt more real than ever before, and Didi wondered if maybe his father had been right when he told his son to spend less time organizing movements and instead invest his creativity in learning how to earn money from the land.

Vania left early each morning so she could drive to other towns, sell lingerie door-to-door, and make it back to Ibiraiaras in time for her afternoon job cutting cauliflower on a rapidly moving conveyor belt. Ivone lost her job as a maid because she insisted on doing things her own way, even in someone else's home. "You're different from every other maid who's worked for me," her employer said. Ivone started working at a stationery store.

In the midst of everything, the family included Dad and me in large, plentiful meals, and Gessi's kids played games and pushed limits just as I had as a kid. Natália attended a public school for free, but Gessi didn't want to take Davi out of the daycare in which she had enrolled him when she had a steady income from the health department. So when money got tight, Gessi, Ivone, and Vania hired themselves out to wash walls in houses around town, a skill Gessi had learned from narrow-minded nuns at a convent when she was fourteen.

Though family life and finances were harder for the whole family after Gessi left the health department, losing that job made space for Gessi to pursue something new. In 2005, she decided to go back to high school and signed up for an adult-education program at Natália's school. Vania enrolled two years later. They attended classes four nights a week for three years. They didn't feel as if they were learning much, but they embraced each assignment and class session, winning over teachers and students who had once insisted that activists had no place in high school classrooms. In the end, the teachers told me, Gessi and Vania had brought "democracy" to the night school class, finding ways to engage other students in projects and decisions. When I asked what they meant by democracy, one teacher said that Gessi, Vania, and other women's movement activists who had come back to school made the classrooms more democratic through their questions. They asked more about the material, pushed back when they disagreed or didn't understand, and, watching them, other students started to do the same.

Amusing moments also came along with being an adult in school—amusing and tough, because they reminded Gessi of gendered expectations that endure. She and I stopped at her school one afternoon to drop off an essay that students had been asked to write for a national contest. The theme of the contest was "Another World Is Possible," a belief Gessi had clung to since she joined the antidam movement in the early 1980s. Gessi's teacher thanked her for handing in the essay, then wondered aloud who should sign the "parent" box on the submission form, since Gessi's father lived an hour away. "Your husband!" the teacher suggested, only half joking. Gessi laughed and signed her own name. To Gessi, the question of how to change the world was much more than an academic one, and she had never waited for permission to take whatever direction she chose.

Two weeks after I graduated from high school, I attended Gessi's graduation. She arrived early to get the props ready for the graduating students' presentation. Like my high school, a performing arts charter school, Gessi's school treated graduation more like a performance than a ceremony. *"Entre!"* Gessi told a nineteen-year-old classmate she found slouched against the building, slapping him on the shoulder. "Enter! It's time to get going." Grudgingly he followed her into a classroom where students whose ages spanned at least thirty years were donning the blue scarves and papier-mâché globes that would serve as their costumes. The chaos and anticipation felt familiar to me. Two weeks earlier, my classmates and I had gathered backstage in the theater where our graduation was held, adjusting caps and gowns and preparing to go onstage. But Gessi's graduation was markedly different from our extravagant one. As I watched Gessi's and Vania's classes perform a play about global warming, staging each scene in a different classroom or hallway of the run-down school, I was struck by how completely Gessi and Vania continued to shape their daily lives around political, environmental, and cultural issues that many of us at home only talked about.

During the same visit, I attended an event honoring Gessi for her recent election as *Conselheira Tutelar,* a coordinator of social services for children and adolescents in Ibiraiaras. In this part-time government position, Gessi and four other women would act as liaisons between local schools, doctors, and families. The mayor began his speech by motioning to the newly elected women. "Men, our troops are dwindling," he told the crowd of government officials and their families. "We will have to participate more in the future." Gessi didn't miss a beat. "You can go work in the kitchen," she quipped, speaking so quietly that only I could hear.

"You're writing only good things about me," Gessi said a few nights later when she finished reading the profile I had written about her. "I have my *defeitos,* my flaws, too, and here," she pointed to the text, which she was reading aloud, "they don't appear." The profile, an early version of chapter 4 of this book, presented the challenges Gessi had faced and overcome, including a father who didn't want her to leave the house, nuns who pushed aside her vision of equality, and leaders of social movements and city government who wouldn't let her fight for change in two places at the same time. But the profile left out what Dad and I had never been able to get at in our interviews with Gessi: what from the safety of her home she now called her defeitos, the places where she, as a person, and not just the world around her, fell short, or didn't know what to do, or just wasn't perfectly on top of things all the time.

Dad had noticed this absence a year earlier when he reread the profile. He was about to speak in the middle school class I was teaching, so we met at a café nearby to prepare. He said the chapter on Gessi seemed too flawless. At first, I didn't know what to say. Gessi seemed that way in person too, I answered, always planning and moving and laughing. So what else was there to write? We couldn't make up flaws. But that's just it, Dad said. Gessi has this incredible energy and charisma that conceals the work it takes to do all she does in the world.

Seated in Gessi's kitchen in 2007, listening to her read aloud from the too-flawless profile, Dad and I learned that she also felt as if something were missing from this telling of her life. Dad responded by talking about our conversation in a café the year before. We can see how much you've done to challenge gender roles and improve local health care, he told Gessi, and the obstacles you've faced, but we don't know what it felt like along the way. We don't know what it took to keep going, to fight against the odds and hold on to a different vision of the world.

When Gessi said we left out her defeitos, we responded, we don't know what they are. We can see the work you do, but it's harder to know what it takes for you to do all that, what it takes out of you. I've thought back to this conversation often, because I grew up thinking that moments of uncertainty or frustration—when you doubt yourself, when you can't clearly see a next step, when you're tired—are defeitos you keep to yourself. And here was Gessi saying, you left out those parts of me, and they're there, and it's okay to let them show.

I hesitated when Dad first encouraged me to share with Ivone and Vania a piece I had written about them. Dad and I had done most of our writing together, leaning over the same computer and arguing about each sentence, or writing independently and editing each other's work. But I had written the profile of Ivone and Vania mostly on my own. Their response to this writing would be a response to me. Reading to Ivone and Vania this mix of our words—their quotes, my narration, their lives, my framing of those lives— meant putting my own ideas on the table in a way I never had before. What if I got the details wrong, or played with Ivone's and Vania's words in a way that made them not want to speak to me? The fear that they would be angered by what I wrote was only part of my hesitation. I was afraid that if I got something wrong, or even if I got something too painfully right, my words would hurt them. And reading aloud my writing—their words and my words, to-gether—was like saying I had a place in their story, which I wasn't sure was true.

I finally asked Ivone and Vania if we could have dinner together, just the three of us, as we had three years earlier. I wanted them to know I had cared enough to write about them, and I wanted to hear their responses to the profile so that I could fix factual errors, add detail, and make my writing more accurately reflect their lives. When I was writing the profile, I used a lot of quotes, so as to let Ivone and Vania speak for themselves. But inevitably at first, and then with excitement, I interpreted their words as well. More diffi-cult was capturing how they are in person: Vania's swift movement and focus in conversation, Ivone's quietness paired with unabashed caring, the offhand, sincere way she told me, "I don't worry about you when you're here," so I shouldn't worry about bothering her when I stopped by in the afternoon to talk. There's a grace to the way Ivone and Vania delve into life, the pride they take in being themselves and the intensity with which they grapple with those selves. Ivone and Vania give the impression of being simultaneously fully formed and wide open, which offered me, as I wrote about them, many points of entry, and many places to go wrong.

Over dinner, they asked after my family and told me about their jobs. Then Vania and I cleared. Ivone never let me wash dishes, but she allowed me to dry. We returned the kitchen to its orderly, comfortable state: dishes put away, leftovers in the refrigerator, extra pots and pans stored in the electric oven. Vania put three logs in the wood stove, and without thinking, we took the same places we had taken three years earlier. Ivone sat on the bench by the stove, and Vania I turned our chairs away from the table to face her. I handed them each a copy of what I had written and began to read aloud.

Reading this profile, which was my telling of the story they had told me, gave way to more stories. Ivone, who always remembered dates, corrected the years I had gotten wrong—but mostly they responded to my writing by adding more. Vania laughed at her own anecdotes and retold them in more detail. This conversation felt deeper than past ones, though it didn't have the same intensity. It didn't make me want to hold my breath, in case I missed a word or asked the wrong question. Our conversations had lost the framework and formality of an interview, and gained a new kind of openness. "*Na verdade, expresas tua opinão*," Ivone said when I read aloud a sentence about what I thought the women's movement meant for rural women. "In fact, you're expressing your opinion." This is a piece about us, she seemed to say, but you're in here too.

A year later, I found myself in their story in a way I didn't know how to be. I had spent the summer doing research at a domestic violence center in northeast Brazil, and I visited Ibiraiaras before going home. Ivone, Vania, and I had dinner and talked about my family, their jobs, and my work in the northeast. And then the table was clear, and Ivone washed and I dried, and she sat on the bench, and Vania propped her feet on the leg of my chair. I had no paper in front of me, no tape recorder, no idea why I had been in Ibiraiaras for days and in the bustle of Gessi's kitchen had yet to see Ivone and Vania exchange a single word.

Vania, who is sometimes gruff and often tired, and who this time had a note of urgency in her voice I hadn't heard before, spoke first. She said, we talk about everything except what happens at home. She said Ivone was turning away from her and every time they speak she feels as if she's done something wrong, as if she owes something, and it's not so much what Ivone says but how she says it that makes the relationship so hard.

If you haven't liked my way of speaking, if you haven't liked it for fourteen years, Ivone said, speaking to Vania even as she looked at me, what kind of person am I? Behind her question were two more that I think Vania and I both heard: What kind of people are we? What kind of people do we want to be? Ivone and Vania stopped talking when I went to the bathroom, but in the kitchen they spoke to each other as much as to me. Vania said, Ivone, you don't look me in the eye when you talk. And Ivone said, I don't have to if I don't want to, and Vania said, you always did.

As I'd worried would happen when I first showed them the profile, it felt as if they were looking to my words to show them something about themselves. At one point the conversation paused and Ivone said, trying to smile, "*E aí, Juíza Emma*"? And you, Judge Emma? I didn't want to be the judge. I was nineteen. I didn't know what it was like to sustain a relationship over decades, to live in a town that won't accept who you are, to start a movement when you're a teenager and see that movement change over time, to gamble on an alternative lifestyle and then no longer have the movement that made that gamble seem possible, to find words failing with the one person with whom you once felt most free. I didn't use my tape recorder or take notes. I listened and, not really knowing how (but maybe having learned from them), tried to sustain a space for them to speak as they had for so many other women.

I learned that night just how much hinges on what can be said. The paradox Ivone and Vania have lived every day, of silence in the space of speech they helped create and the need to draw curtains around themselves in the place they call home, would have been easy to overlook if not for the dinners I had there. Even knowing that there was no place for Ivone and Vania to speak about their relationship outside the walls of their home, I saw many times what a vibrant space of conversation that home could be. I saw that alternative visions of the world make space for alternative realities, and that when people bet on new paths, when Ivone and Vania form a relationship that their society, their comrades in a women's movement, and their family next door can tolerate but not accept, what's at stake is not only their day-to-day lives but also their continued commitment to activism.

"We want democracy, we want equality, we want and we want and we want," Vania told me. "But when it comes time to speak, in practice it's you who has to say what you need to say." She and Ivone helped found the women's movement to fight for rural women like themselves, but their own selves were silenced along the way. When it comes down to it, Vania said finally, it's you who must speak. You can't fight for others to be recognized as people without speaking up for yourself. Leaders, no matter how dedicated and no matter how strong, also need to *ser gente*, to be people in the fullest sense of the word: people with strong voices, legal citizenship, and the right to create and take on new roles.

What was it like for Ivone, Vania, and Gessi to see my collaboration with my father? I still don't know for sure, but moments and comments have given me clues. I once asked Ivone what she thought when Dad and I first did research in Ibiraiaras together. Speaking for herself and other women, Ivone said, "We hoped it could become possible in Brazil someday for fathers and daughters to work like that." By doing research together, Dad and I brought part of our lives to Ibiraiaras, so that we were not the anonymous researchers we could have been on our own. Just as we noticed how women interacted with their families, they watched our interactions, noting the moments when we teased each other, argued, or worked together to communicate an idea.

What they couldn't watch, because they only knew us there, were the ways in which their battles for voice and citizenship resonate in the United States as well. I have not faced the hard-and-fast walls that were just beginning to break as women like my mom pursued careers in medicine, or that Elenice faced when she decided to go back to school. As a recent college graduate, there are no careers that seem off limits to me, no spaces in which I have been told I have no right to speak. But that is not a given, not for women younger than me, like my sisters, as they head into middle school and college, and not for me going forward. The traditions Brazilian women began to challenge when they founded the women's movement—who speaks, who makes decisions, who does the dishes—also have a deep hold here.

Like me, Ivone got interested in her father's work before she knew what her own work would be. So in some ways, her father, who fought for union reform, was a model for the kind of activist she wanted to become. But in other ways, he stood in the way of her becoming the kind of person she wanted to be—someone who could leave the house, join social movements, speak at the dinner table—because he believed that women belonged at home.

Plenty of *defeitos* come out of my collaboration with my father, moments of misunderstanding or frustration, and times when Dad wanted to work together and I was wrapped up in college or had my head in the next thing I wanted to do. Dad and I really talk to each other, and that means there are moments when we disagree. Ivone didn't see all of those moments, because when Dad and I are not in Ibiraiaras, we're far away. Still, despite—or perhaps, because—of the mix of defeitos and excitement that she does see, I think Ivone saw in Dad and me a way of working together that she had been working toward when she tried to explain to her father why a women's movement was necessary, and when she defied him to start one, hoping that he would someday listen to what she had to say. If, for Ivone, Dad and I were an example of what she was fighting for, we were also a reminder of what she, as a teenager, most wanted and didn't have.

"When you speak of changes," Ivone told Dad and me, "I think of my father." Was she talking about the father who had stood in her way? Or about the father who had changed, who now supported his daughters' activism and spoke about Ivone and Gessi with pride as he showed Dad and me around the house where he raised them? I sensed a kind of bittersweetness in Ivone's comment about her father, and I realized that the same mixed emotions— sadness, hope, uncertainty, pride—may come along with watching Dad and me. Maybe that's what Dad's former graduate student Laura Roush meant when she told him her reaction to our collaboration, which she has followed since it started nine years ago. When she hears about our project, she told Dad, she thinks of her relationship with her father.

Our collaboration, and not just our questions, made Gessi, Ivone, Vania, and the other women we met in Brazil reflect on their own lives, just as watching them made Dad and me reflect on our own. They treated us not just as American researchers, or as a father-daughter team, but also as two individuals who are, in our own ways, enchanted by the work they are doing.

Watching Gessi, Ivone, and Vania in 2007 and 2008, in moments shaped by sadness and by possibility, I saw some of the things they said I had left out of their profiles: for Gessi, the uncertainties, the defeitos she feels, and for Ivone and Vania, their continued longing for a relationship not bound by silence. I realized that from the first time Gessi said she had "two hearts," she wasn't talking only about a political decision or a choice about what work shaped her days. She was also saying something about how it feels to try to make change, and to figure out where you fit in. And when Ivone and Vania spoke about trying to find spaces of speech amid silence, and let me in on a moment when they felt as if that space was gone, it was still with the hope that speech could be maintained.

Perhaps because Gessi, Ivone, and Vania threw themselves so fully into the women's movement when they were my age, there's something deeply personal about the way they approach their work, as if they have a heightened sense of what's at stake in how they live their lives. If you start a women's movement so you can speak in your own home, how can any work you later do on gender or politics not feel personal? You have to care deeply to start something as a teenager, and you have to continue caring to sustain your commitment to what that activism was about, even when it's not part of your life anymore.

For me, this project has opened up new questions about how I want to live my life. For Gessi, Ivone, and Vania, the question of where to fight for change, and how to enact at home the values around which they once formed a movement, hasn't gone away. If anything, it has become less clear, and part of the drive that has always struck me about these women comes from their continuing desire to change the world.

MOVEMENTS IN DEMOCRACY
Jeff

In one of the lessons in our curriculum, we use video interviews with the women of the MMTR to get students talking about what it means to form a movement. At the end of a class we taught to sixth graders in Massachusetts, a student who had barely spoken all year, according to her teacher, summed up the lively discussion. The student spoke softly and intently, much as the women in Ibiraiaras might speak at a meeting, and her teacher leaned in from the back of the room to hear. "Each woman," the student said, bringing her hands from beneath her desk and folding them neatly on its surface, "is motivated by one thing, but they all connect to women's rights. Gessi's is being a leader and getting women's rights. Mônica wants rights, but she also wants to help her family. Elenice, she wants an education, and she wants rights. And it all combines together, and if all women do that, they're probably going to get rights, if they keep working at it. They can't give up."

In preparing to bring our curriculum back to Brazil in 2007, we gathered together everything we could find related to the curriculum itself and the teaching we had done with it. To a binder overflowing with lesson plans we added letters to the women from students who had taken the course, photos of workshops we'd run for teachers, and videos of classes, such as the one in which the sixth grader had so aptly captured the multiple aims of the women in the MMTR. Before leaving the United States, Emma and I considered the obstacles that shape the work of field researchers as they move back and forth transnationally, from the unequal power of researcher and subject to the hubris of studying and interpreting the inner workings of a group to which one does not belong.[1] When you hand someone a piece of writing or a lesson plan that says, "Here is your life," there is no response you can or should be able to count on.

In my previous travels and research, I had encountered warmth and mutuality, understanding these as gifts one has to look for and earn. I gained knowledge from those with whom I achieved an ongoing and shared pleasure in analyzing the world. But these interactions told only part of the story. In the detective work that is ethnography, key insights follow from games of cat and mouse, adversarial conversations, suspicions, denials, and surprises. In Sananduva and Ibiraiaras people were willing to talk to me from the beginning, but I

Women's movement meeting. *Photograph by Jeffrey W. Rubin.*

heard the same story over and over again. Then as things began to change, I brought my daughter with me, and we moved together beyond the official story of the women's movement to the more-subtle and even contradictory ways that gender and politics entered women's daily lives.

When we returned with the curriculum in 2007, we presented our work to women in the same kitchens and union halls where we had first learned about their organizing and ideas. They thought the curriculum was subversive in its aim of exposing students to activism, and they saw how much work had gone into it. "Look what Jeffrey and Emma have done," we heard over and over. This was especially gratifying since until we created one ourselves, we had no idea what went into producing a secondary school curriculum. Only now do I begin to understand the interconnected tasks of coming up with ideas, translating them into lessons, learning from everyone you can get to talk to you, and transforming all of that into a physical product, with tabs and a binder, unit outlines and lesson plans, so that you can place it in people's hands and they can use it to teach.

The day after we arrived, with the plastic floral centerpiece back in the center of Gessi's table after lunch, the laundry folding on hold, and the warm winter sun pouring through the corner windows, we had a few minutes all together:

Gessi, Ivone, Vania, Emma, and I. As always, we plunged into discussion of matters at hand, usually recent events in Ibiraiaras or the women's movement, Brazilian politics, or work and family life. This time, however, it was our curriculum. These were the people close to us who had given us their time and stories. We were telling their history, and we didn't know how they would respond.

Our conversation surged forward with examples and questions. The five of us share a love of curiosity, of uncovering experience and interpreting it. As we explained the curriculum materials, Gessi gestured animatedly, exploring each new image and technique. Ivone's inflection was one of cautious emotion, and Vania grinned, perceiving the key points instantly. Emma and I careened through our presentation, peppering the videos and lesson outlines with our favorite anecdotes. Whenever we saw puzzlement, we rushed in to explain, going back to the origins of whatever question or image in a lesson had caught their attention and telling them how we had come upon it. They listened closely, repeating and playing out the details of how we'd designed the curriculum and where we'd taught it, making our story their own. We could see Gessi remembering the phrases and anecdotes she liked best—much as we had in past interviews with her—so that she could get the word out in town.

A few days later, in the union hall in Sananduva, the MMTR women we'd met over the years there gathered around our laptop, watching videos of themselves that we used in our lessons. "You're there!" one of the women exclaimed, as Rosane watched herself explaining that men were also happier when they took a role in running the household. Then the women spread out in chairs around the wide meeting table, the same table where I had faced an exhausted Vera at the end of a long day of union work years before. After Emma and I walked the women through the materials, they discussed the curriculum and the women's movement, proceeding one to the next around the table. The last woman to speak, the youngest among them, leaned forward, opening her hands. "My God, I also lived this," she told the group. "But we didn't save anything . . . a photo here, a photo there, like souvenirs."

Even without a local archive, the women in the women's movement were organizers. It is their work to gather and present information effectively, and to get to the heart of things, and they recognized this aspect of their work in our own. Perhaps that is part of what their tears meant, and their curious but never hard-hitting questions, as they watched images of themselves speaking to American students. In using their words to teach about women's activism, we were also bringing them documentation of their history. "It's a concrete thing you've done," Rosane said, "showing something that really happened. You're taking to the United States concrete and practical experiences that we created here."

Emma and I remember key moments in the process of mixing our words with those of women from Rio Grande do Sul, how we learned to think together, with the women and each other, back and forth over what has become years. This closeness was not there from the beginning; it had to be made. We can picture the moments when that happened with Gessi, Ivone, and Vania, moments of excitement or sadness in discussing their paths in the MMTR, as well as personal moments, when one of us asked advice and the others didn't know exactly how to answer, but went ahead and mused aloud. We take pleasure in these exchanges, when the other person knows where your idea is going and grabs it and takes it further, or even connects it to something entirely different. And what it means—what does it mean?—for a father and daughter and women who fled their fathers (to return on different terms) to pursue ideas together and bring them to tangible fruition.

When we returned with our curriculum in 2007, conversations in Ivone and Vania's kitchen took on a more personal tone than in previous visits. As always, this was the most comfortable place for me in Ibiraiaras. During our family year in Brazil, when I had stayed in Ivone and Vania's house with Shoshana and our daughters, the kitchen was our center of operations. It was summer then, and hot, and this was where we sipped cold drinks, coordinated our activities, and chatted together at the end of the day. When I returned with Emma in winter on our research trip, this was the one room in Ibiraiaras where I felt warm and completely at ease the moment I entered, with the flowered curtains drawn and the table set, thick vegetable soup and steaming polenta just off the stove, and Ivone and Vania putting the finishing touches on dinner and table setting and settling in to greet us. This time, returning with the curriculum in a milder winter, it seemed a plain kitchen, the objects simply objects: small Formica counters, glass slats on the windows, shiny metal chairs with plastic cushions. The key now was the ease of conversation and the sense of trust and familiarity.

When Emma and I discussed the conversations we had with Ivone and Vania during this visit, and a follow-up visit a year later, we realized that they were willing to try out their ideas on us, and Emma felt the same way toward them.

She was willing to express uncertainty to the two women; as she said, "to try to say something beyond my language ability." That means, I came to think later, communicating to others something you are only beginning to feel and know yourself, so that you are in dialogue with them about your most inti mate knowledge. That's what the women in the movement are reaching toward themselves when they speak over and over about dialogue, when dialogue itself becomes their imaginary of development. Emma told me that this research on the women's movement and the relationships she had with the women in Ibiraiaras showed her "an alternative to home."

What else had Emma learned? "I've learned to trust my instincts more with other people," she told me in Ibiraiaras. "In a way, to be someone people can trust."

When Emma was twelve and saw the power of the women in the church basement in Santa Lucia, she had wanted to get more inside it. When we returned together to do research for the curriculum, she wanted to be able to represent the events of the women's movement in writing and teach about them to middle and high school students. Now, returning to another meeting to show the women our curriculum, Emma felt—and liked feeling—simultaneously on the inside and the outside, switching easily from filming to participating and even doing both at the same time. Her flexibility was saying something beyond her language ability. And that's what our father-daughter collaboration has done: taught us how to live in the world in a new way.

As a professor, I have crossed a border. When our project began, I saw my scholarly research and teaching on one side and the curriculum project with Emma on the other. We said then that Emma would translate me for a broader (and younger) audience. But that's not what happened. It turns out that the learning and creativity go in both directions in a way that fundamentally changes my notion of university teaching and scholarship—and being a parent. Our neighbor Mary Jo Salter, a poet and teacher, has followed our project since its inception. After reading our first portraits of women in the MMTR, she told us, "You teach your children—teach a lot of things—by teaching about what you know, sharing what you are excited about. You teach your children by learning from them and in some sense letting them know that. That means you are listening."

There are rules for being a teacher that I follow automatically with my students. I would never say to a student "that's a dumb answer" or "why in the world did you do it that way?" Being a parent is much more complicated, of course, and despite my best intentions, at home I say things like this all the time. In my project with Emma, I tempered the emotions of parenting—and the seemingly male insistence inside me that makes patience and understanding difficult in the pressured moments of daily life—with a set of procedures I had learned in the classroom. This enabled me to learn to observe and to write from my daughter.

At the first meeting we attended together on our joint research trip, the kickoff to the mayoral campaign in Ibiraiaras, Emma noticed who sat where in the room and how Gessi crossed and recrossed the invisible boundaries between men and women with ease. Emma registered who spoke with authority and with what gestures, while I focused on interpreting speeches and the political implications of what each person said. I knew how to analyze words, and my daughter knew what was happening in the room. In addition to observing with more nuance than I did, Emma wrote more fluidly, bringing her sense of scene and narrative directly into her prose. In contrast, I struggled with beginnings, with getting ideas down on paper in an initial draft, but loved to revise. In the early stages of our collaboration, we would brainstorm for hours about a particular person and then agree at some point that it was time for Emma to write. She'd settle on a couch or bed, groaning about how difficult it was to put into words what we had discussed and often staying up late into the night to work out a difficult passage. But she'd have a complete first draft by the next morning.

This division of labor changed after our return with our curriculum, when we left Ibiraiaras for a week of writing in an old fishing cottage by the water. The coast of Santa Catarina, one of Brazil's southernmost states, was gray and cold, with only occasional flashes of sun. The cottage, white with bright-red doors and shutters, was always chilly. With portable space heaters by our feet, we began by following our usual routine, discussing a subject first, followed by Emma writing and me revising. But halfway through the week, I started waking up earlier than Emma. Padding into the living room in my pajamas and fleece, I carefully pushed open the shutters and watched the fishermen head out in their long boats as the sky lightened. I glanced into Emma's room and felt the quiet pleasure of having brought her to this magical place. I brewed tea and sat by the window with my laptop. Then, over the course of half an hour, I moved from revising what Emma had written to writing new passages. And in those passages I described what scenes looked like and how people moved within them.

If our research and writing benefited from combining the emotions of family life with the procedural habits of teaching, the mix brought risks as well. It both strengthened and limited our capacity to argue, in Brazil and at home. "I felt if we argued," Emma told me later, "about cleaning the kitchen or taking care of my sisters or about the book, then the project would fall apart." Another time when Emma reflected on our work together, she told me she liked that she could argue about our work. She said, "I knew you wouldn't give in to me if you didn't agree." This made sense to me, because I knew how often I gave in to Emma in our family life, stretching the boundaries of what I myself wanted or thought reasonable to accommodate her wishes. When I told Emma this, she said that wasn't her impression: "In high school I was always holding back on what I wanted at home, not wanting to push."

Outside of our collaboration, I've realized, we were both second-guessing ourselves. We were afraid of saying what we were really thinking. By comparison, collaborating on research was generally straightforward. "I think I gained or found skills and ways of interacting through this that I didn't necessarily have a model for elsewhere," Emma told me. "That you can be close and also be thoughtful and separate and disagree and hand off tasks, that you can argue as part of the project, as making the project more exciting. It's interesting to me that I'm so willing to argue with you, to get annoyed."

"Maybe there's something we both like about being in that space of risk and uncertainty," she added. "I can be really strong in this without running you over."

Emma's capacity for argument was legendary in our family and had long been a staple in her relationship with Shoshana and me. As new parents, we found it hard to say no, especially with our oldest daughter, and Emma became an expert, from age one or two, at getting what she wanted. "Is that the kind of no that means no?" she asked once as we pushed her in a stroller in front of a demolition site in New York City, her voice clear and firm through the ear-splitting noise, "or is that the kind of no where if I say I want it again and again, you'll let me?"

Doing research and writing together, we argued the merits. In contrast to the kinds of indirect arguments that often happen in families, we were "fighting fair": saying what we meant, sticking to our guns, and mentally and verbally duking it out.

We anguished over some key decisions, such as the voice in which we would write. In the fishing cottage in Santa Catarina, we consciously continued what we had begun without a thought when we returned from our first research trip in 2004—writing together in one voice. We were inventing an "I," a joint observer who would represent both of us as we figured out what we were learning and how to communicate it. We would be honest with our readers, revealing the dual identities behind the single voice. Behind the question of "I" and "we" lay a deeper problem, however: how were we to convey the back and forth of our ongoing dialogue? It wasn't really that we completed each other's thoughts, as friends and teachers at our workshops saw it. Rather, our distinct thoughts raced into and around each other, morphing in the process, and what people heard was the result. Mary Ellen Miller, Emma's clarinet teacher, pressed us to think of our collaboration as a duet. But how do you communicate accessibly, in writing, the intertwining of voices? Eventually we realized that we needed to write in two voices, that our dialogue would occur through chapters. What surprises us now is how difficult it was to reach this conclusion and how long it took us to leave the imagined "I"—and with it one of our ways of being a family—behind.

I also left behind conventional notions of scholarship. I gained the insights I did into the politics of activism because my daughter accompanied me as a co-researcher; women responded to our relationship and to her in explaining their political and personal actions. One evening Emma asked Ivone and Vania what they thought when I first arrived, a male researcher from the United States wanting to study a women's movement. She joked that maybe I should leave the room so they could tell the truth. I laughed and walked out the door. Research isn't usually done in teams, and being there together let us ask questions about each other that we couldn't have asked about ourselves. It was late and cold and I stayed outside for only a moment. But once she started talking, Vania was happy to finish her story with me in the room. She spoke about not knowing at first whether to trust me, if I would indeed come back more than once and if she would want to have me around. I did come back, soon after, with my whole family in tow. Ivone said how much it mattered that we stayed in their house and ate meals with them during that family visit. That week I wasn't a researcher carefully finding my way in, she said, but a real person with a fun and demanding family. Vania remembered the full house that week, "two families with their own schedules and needs and organization." She recalled arriving one day to see me leaning into the refrigerator and vividly remembered my response to her presence. "Our things were all over the place," I told her, "so I organized the refrigerator."

Over the course of nine years, Emma and I have taken our work back and forth to the women in the MMTR, to secondary school and university classrooms in

Brazil and the United States, and to family members and friends, engaging in dialogue that extends outward from the university both transnationally and locally. What we know has grown out of the observations of women and men, teachers and students, in all of these locations, talking to us and to each other. In this circuitous dialogue, ideas that Emma and I developed to simplify ethnographic material for secondary school students have become the theoretical underpinnings of our scholarly analysis. We first used the idea of paradox to capture a central characteristic of each woman about whom we wrote, so she could represent one aspect of the women's movement to students. This worked for teaching, but then paradox went further for us, pressed in new directions by new interlocutors. We realized that the paradoxes we identified were lived as tensions, bringing personal and collective history into the present, and these acute discomforts pressed women to act. Paradoxes, a long-time observer of our collaboration suggested, gave movement to movements, pressed them to bring the future into being as they moved through time.[2] And the idea of paradox presented the notion of "holding" as well, the holding of paradox that gives depth to musical performance, as Mary Ellen illustrated, and also makes it hard for an individual to stay in a movement while balancing irresolvable tensions and hard for a movement itself to hold many different kinds of people.

When we taught a workshop at Duke University for sixth-grade social studies teachers, we invited Wendy Wolford, then a professor in the geography department at the University of North Carolina and an expert on the MST, to join us and say a bit about the history of the struggle for land in Brazil. When Wendy saw the way we used interview clips to teach about the women's movement, she connected her own research and teaching in a new way. "I do interviews all the time," she told us, "but I've never thought of using them in my classes." The following semester, Wendy designed a research and methodology course for graduate students titled "Ethnographies of Globalization." In putting the course together, she asked scholars of different parts of the world to submit an interview transcript, a description of the context in which the interview took place, and a published article that resulted from the interview. The course, inspired by the inductive methods of our curriculum, used interviews to teach graduate students simultaneously about compelling world issues and how scholars do research.

When Emma and I spoke in my Latin American history class at Boston University about the way our styles of observation had been so different at the start of our collaboration, one young woman shouted from the back of the lecture hall, "That's because you're a guy and she's a girl." The class laughed, surprised by the student's audacity and apparent accuracy. The truth was more complicated. When we started doing research together in 2004, Emma and I were father and daughter, professor and student, seasoned ethnographer and young traveler. Years later, however, we have ceased noticing different kinds of detail in predictable ways. And we've changed in our interaction with each other, becoming research partners in addition to parent and child. The changes in our relationship brought us to the center of the women's movement and the conflicted hearts of the women who formed it.

At the International Women's Day meeting in the gymnasium in 2002, with women from all the different social movements gathered together—after the day-long lectures on the Brazilian economy, the women holding on to the microphone to tell their stories, the pageantry of socialism as a seeming Garden of Eden—Olivio Dutra, the governor of the state of Rio Grande do Sul at the time, arrived to address the gathering in the enormous gym, ringed on the inside by the concrete bleachers where the women rested and slept and the outside by the tents where they cooked and ate and gossiped. At this moment, Gessi introduced the governor simply: "We need to move forward so that the state will fulfill its promises, so that social movements will achieve their place and know where power is, and so that gender will be taken seriously and be more than a discourse." This eloquent introduction at the center of a highly orchestrated meeting bespoke Gessi's skill, the same skill she had used to impress the priests with her "diplomacy" years before. She placed before the governor the essence of the women's movement's hopes and demands. But when I thought about it later, I realized these remarks struck a surprisingly open-ended note. What *is* the place of social movements, and where is power? Gessi, like Vera, knows how complicated and dangerous power can be. She knows that as a leader of the women's movement she supported the majority view and the ousting of others and that she in turn was marginalized when she opted to run the health department and work within the institutions. Now Gessi agrees with Vera that there shouldn't have to be only one viewpoint in a movement, that there should be what she has come to call flexibility.

Vera calls it autonomy and connects it to the sense of self the MMTR fought to develop in women since its inception, what she calls *o meu eu* (my I). Vera left the women's movement the moment that she felt self-denigrated, though now she thinks she should have fought back to make a place for voice and dissent. As an outsider, I've come to believe that what's at stake is the very possibility of a "movement in democracy," a mobilized, grassroots force for change that acts in, around, and through electoral and legislative procedures. Movements in democracy are something the world needs very much at this moment, as authoritarian regimes across the globe give way to democratic forms of government. And they're something that the women in the MMTR have reached for in the course of their activism. The idea of movement in democracy grew out of my conversations with the women over the past fifteen years as I've tried to figure out what caused so many of them to distance themselves from the headquarters of the women's movement and follow their own diverging trajectories of activism.

I've followed debates in the women's movement about doing politics in the streets or in the institutions and arguments about forging one unified position or allowing internal pluralism, all of this while Brazil has functioned politically as a democracy at national and local levels. And I've followed the lives of many of the women and the outsiders who have advised them—priests, professors, other feminists—as they've grappled with questions about the place of movements in democracies and reached similar conclusions, though at different times and in different ways. All of them, as activists, have spent much of two decades in an effort to change the world around them—literally *re-form* that world—in significant and enduring ways.

The moment of possibility of one women's movement containing multiple women, projects, views, and strategies is gone. But many women can now envision a flexible kind of movement, a movement of deeply connected yet autonomous individuals, some of them doing battle within the institutions of Brazil's democracy, in the health departments and schools, the city councils and town halls, and the political parties and electoral commissions, and others outside of them, in the neighborhoods, in the land occupations and the Pilgrimages for the Land, outside the doors of government offices, in the alternative pharmacies, and in the streets. One women's movement holding and enabling different viewpoints, strategies, and emotions.

Why the pressure to separate, to choose one over the other, the streets or the institutions, the centralization of militant national organizations like the MST or the diverse reformist efforts under way in local governments? Why not understand power as Vera suggested to me in the union hall early on, as something transitory that needs to be shared, not centralized, within a movement? Or as Rosane put it, "Why can't some of us in the women's movement support the union and others support the MST?" It isn't simply that democracy and elections lead people to run for office or take government jobs, so that there is less pressure for change from marches and demonstrations, with their edge of anger and threat. What's also hard about movements in democracy is balancing speech and disagreement within the very organizations that provide alternative visions for the future.

And what happens when gender moves beyond discourse, when challenging the practices resulting from gender inequalities moves to the center of politics and daily life, as Gessi suggested to the governor? Like Izanete and Ivone and the women at the pharmacy, Gessi knows how hard it is to go door to door, literally and figuratively, to try and convince women to see the world in a new way. She has seen over years how hard it is to change men's attitudes and beliefs, their refusals and violence. She also knows that at particular moments, dramatic public mobilizations can press legislators to turn women's economic needs into legal rights. Like Vera, Gessi knows that she's not sure what she means when she imagines a future without the constraints of gender —who would people be?—though she *is* sure that women should have voice and decision-making power in every domain of their lives. And like the women in the pharmacy and at the meeting in Santa Lucia, Gessi knows the pain and hardship of women's daily lives, the intractability of gender roles inside women themselves and all around them, and the reality of hard-won change.

Gessi and the women in the rural women's movement are fighting for more than rights in any conventional sense. Bringing gender to the center of politics means you have to grapple day in and day out with what it means to change— and fail to change—those you know and love. If you stay home and fight for equality and voice for women, you are fighting to redeem the past as much as to create the future, to reach what might have been and might yet be. In her lifelong commitment to *luta* (struggle), Gessi is fighting for a better way of living she can't define and a way of holding power she has not experienced.

I think what Gessi said to the governor contained both her strength and her uncertainty, the fault lines of what she doesn't know that run deeply through her conviction about the need for change. That's real diplomacy, deftly showing to others your skills while allowing room to maneuver. Gessi would recognize the question I come back to again and again, because I've come to frame it the way I do as I've followed the history of the MMTR and the women in it. How, I wonder, in a world of economic harms and religious fundamentalisms, of wrenching poverty and horrific violence, can there be created—by whom, by what?—spaces for people to ser gente, in Izanete's words, to know themselves as fully human and have the political rights and voice and economic well-being that being human and equal entails?

The statewide women's movement, with its headquarters in a well-tended house in Passo Fundo, answers that question by insisting on the need for a single movement strategy. At the end of our trip in 2007, Emma and I visited the headquarters to present copies of our curriculum to the movement's current leaders. In the course of a long afternoon, our conversation went far beyond the curriculum, and we left with new insight into questions about the movement's history and political choices that we'd been wondering about for years.

At the headquarters, Emma and I were surprised to encounter two women very different from Adriana and Salete, the MMTR leaders in their early forties with whom we had talked three years earlier. One of the women who greeted us this time, Mariane Martins, was younger than Adriana and Salete, and the other, Sister Carminha Lorenzoni, was older. Mariane, who went by Mari, greeted us at the door with courtesy and some reservation. Mari, a new leader of the MMTR who had been educated in schools run jointly with the MST and other movements, had not met us before and knew little about our curriculum project. But we had interacted with Carminha, one of the nuns who had supported the women's movement since its inception, numerous times at movement events, and she greeted us warmly. Carminha's enthusiastic hugs won over her younger colleague, who proved to be sharp and articulate and was able seamlessly to connect the ideology of the women's movement to recent political events.

When I think now about what made our project work—what moment-to-moment decisions, often unconscious, led the women to trust us—I remember my first conversation with Carminha at the women's movement statewide assembly in 2001, after dinner had been cleared and the dishes washed. As soon as she learned that I was from the United States, Carminha engaged me in a discussion of 9/11, which had happened just two months before. In the darkening tent, Carminha briefly acknowledged the sadness of so many deaths and then went on to suggest that there was considerable benefit to the

United States experiencing itself as vulnerable to violence and destruction, the way so much of the world already was. Instead of agreeing, I responded by speaking of the innocent victims of the 9/11 attack, many of them janitors and firefighters, and about our friends and family in New York. I'm not sure why I refused the easy step from distress over innocent victims to condemnation of the U.S. government's own violence abroad. Agreeing with Carminha and others on the left in Brazil who asked similar questions about 9/11 might have opened doors to the movements I wanted to get to know, and their observations about U.S. power were true enough, particularly from a Latin American perspective. My own emotions played a role here, along with a commitment to honesty that went beyond the literal meaning of what I said to an expression of my own evolving feelings and beliefs. I wanted from the beginning to be engaged in a dialogue with the women whose movement I studied, and Carminha was a willing partner as I thought aloud through my own responses to her assertions. Emma, in the early stages of learning Portuguese at the time, did not understand all of the details of our conversation, but she noted with surprise the absence of tension as Carminha and I discussed the controversial topic.

As soon as we arrived with the curriculum, Mari and Carminha excitedly told us about the women's movement's latest major mobilization, carried out with women from other movements in the state. On International Women's Day in 2006, the women had invaded the state headquarters of agricultural giant Aracruz Inc. and destroyed genetically modified crops to protest the expansion of eucalyptus plantations in Rio Grande do Sul. This act of civil disobedience further distanced those who had left the statewide organization but remained active on women's issues primarily in their towns, such as Gessi, Vera, Rosane, and Mônica, from women who continued to be affiliated with the movement headquarters in Passo Fundo. The women who worked only on local issues now found it hard to get news of friends who had joined in the protests. When we said we wanted to visit the headquarters, they didn't know its new phone number or location and didn't seem willing or able to call around and find out. At the same time, as a result of its dramatic tactics and the forceful police response, the MMTR garnered considerable international attention and solidarity, which Mari and Carminha recounted with pride.

Many of the people to whom we spoke about the Aracruz protest oppose the destruction of property and think the movement went too far, for any number of reasons: by breaking the law, by choosing the wrong issue, by taking dramatic action without preparing the groundwork in public opinion, or by subsuming their struggle for women's rights to the goals of movements more concerned with inequalities of land ownership and corporate agriculture, like the MST and Via Campesina, the international coalition of rural movements. However, almost no one we knew in Brazil who supported progressive causes would condemn the decisions of the women's movement headquarters outright, and all of them examined the movement's actions and their context with considerable open-mindedness. Such is the nature of the fight for social justice in Brazil. There is very little certainty about what works, and those who don't subscribe to a particular orthodoxy see value in both radical activism and everyday politics. In addition, some of the people sympathetic to electoral politics and government remain open to radical tactics because they feel that Lula's and Dilma's administrations—the culmination of their twenty-year path from the streets to the institutions as dictatorship gave way to democracy—have brought economic growth without challenging Brazil's vastly unequal systems of property and power.

I pressed Carminha, who has long been involved with the women's movement, and Mari, who remembers taking notes for her mother at movement meetings when she was a child, on the question of what Gessi calls flexibility. I listed the many women we have spoken to who are no longer active in the statewide movement, even though they continue supporting movement initiatives and other women's campaigns in their towns. Each of these women we knew had opted in one way or another for the institutions, taking leadership roles in unions or local governments, at the same time that the leaders of the women's movement had chosen to ally with the MST and Via Campesina, with their stress on protest in the streets and head-on confrontation with governments and landowners. These political decisions had engendered great personal rancor and, ultimately, sadness. More than once we were shown photo albums filled with snapshots of many of the women we knew all together at weddings, baptisms, graduations, and protests. Now they gained news of one another from a distance and acknowledged this with nostalgia and a deep sense of loss.

Three years earlier, Adriana and Salete responded cautiously when we raised these issues, willing to state that joining the government meant leaving the movement, but deflecting our questions about the implications of such a stance. Now Carminha and Mari were warmer and more direct. They explained that to believe in unions and local governments is a very different thing from believing in a project of radical social change. "And if you understand that," Mari went on, "then you understand that you have to make a choice."

In response, I put into words something I had been thinking about for a long time, and in so doing played a more active role in the conversation than I had in my previous interviews with activists. As a foreigner and an ethnographer, I generally let my questions follow or fit within the words of others, pressing gently against borders and noting how they shift. But now I said, "It sounds like you were willing to lose key leaders so that you could join with a larger and more radical political project." This was something I more or less knew to be true and indeed had learned a good deal about over the years, but had rarely addressed head-on. To say these words, with their formal and measured cadence, was to acknowledge that I was crossing a line. And for Carminha and Mari to respond without missing a beat was to accept that crossing.

Carminha nodded, though she didn't volunteer details about the circumstances under which women she knew well had left the MMTR. Mari was more direct: "It's about what's fundamental, the character of the movement." In explaining what she meant, Mari spoke generally at first, observing that movements change, that some leaders leave and others come in. Her remarks ignored the pain and nostalgia we encountered whenever we talked with women we knew about the history of the movement or its current strategies. Mari also downplayed the purposefulness with which decisions had been made and opposing voices outmaneuvered. But Mari and Carminha seemed open to my question. They went on to acknowledge that women didn't just leave the MMTR for personal reasons, owing to their life trajectories, but were forced out in various ways, and that joining Via Campesina was a political decision with benefits and real losses.

"They actually said that?" Elenice responded, taken aback, when I recounted the conversation afterward in her living room. Mari's and Carminha's remarks were made on the record—we videotaped the interview for future use in the curriculum project—and I repeated them because Elenice and I had discussed these issues frankly before. Gessi was similarly startled when I returned from Passo Fundo and, in response to questions about what had been discussed there, told her and her family about Mari's and Carminha's comments. I was in turn surprised by Gessi's immediate and palpable distress, as she quickly got up from the dinner table and turned to change Davi's diaper. For me, Mari and Carminha's summary of the movement's current strategy confirmed what I had begun to learn years before from Elenice and Gessi themselves. But to the two founders of the movement, who had been forced out with no discussion, these words were devastating. To this day I am not sure whether I should have repeated them.

Joining Via Campesina, I had come to understand over time, like joining the MST, meant privileging militant challenge to the economic status quo over both gender concerns and incremental reform within the system. In addition, in Rio Grande do Sul, the internal politics of both organizations favored hierarchy, with decisions made at the top.[3] The MST, like the Catholic Church —the same forces that had fostered speech and political activism among the young people of Rio Grande do Sul in the first place—sought to limit voice and disagreement in the name of a utopian future. For leftists in the Leninist tradition, challenging power meant enforcing rules of unity so as to mobilize swiftly, with the force of masses. That seemed the only way to stand a chance against the vast power of national governments and the global economy. But theorizing at the top took little account of the pain Gessi and Elenice masked in the instant between their gasps of surprise and their quickly turning to other tasks.

I spoke explicitly to Mari and Carminha for several reasons, not least of which was my sense, as the interview progressed, that I could do so without endangering my formal relationship with the headquarters and my access to the leaders there. I sensed that the space had been created for such a question, as it had for my repeating their remarks to Gessi and Elenice. I also spoke directly, in both instances, because the issue of exclusion so affected the women we knew in Sananduva and Ibiraiaras and because it was one of the main stories of the women's movement itself, one I had worked hard to understand. And by now the issue of silence amid speech was central to the way Emma and I understood the lives of women and the way they partici-pated in movements.

Gessi and other past leaders no longer go to the women's movement head-quarters, and if they ventured there, they would not be met with the same reception we gained as persistent foreign researchers. Our presence was useful to the movement because the leaders faced criminal charges as a result of the Aracruz protest, and the MMTR had survived the controversial action due to international support. In addition, we brought a complete curriculum on social movements in Brazil that featured the women's movement and its ally, the MST. As we exchanged our materials for movement pamphlets and posters, alive with imagery of smiling and purposeful rural women fighting for social and economic change, it was painful for us to realize how willingly the current leaders of MMTR, who had begun winning elections for the movement's executive committee in the mid-1990s, had forced Gessi and others out. Losing leaders—and losing friends—was part of their battle for radical change.

Gessi remains sympathetic to the MMTR's militancy and the current leaders' insistence that activists adopt a common stance. Gessi herself had supported the ousting of women who pressed for a diversity of approaches within the MMTR. But now Gessi knows she isn't welcome at the movement headquarters and that the leaders there don't accept the work that she sees as a valuable contribution to a shared vision. Still, she organizes the women's movement in her town and displays the MMTR flag at local meetings. She introduces herself as an activist in the movement, unwilling to turn her back on a struggle in which she continues to believe. Reflecting on the process by which the women's movement enforced unity, Gessi says, "We always made decisions that others didn't like when I was a leader of the movement. I just wish they would tell me why they're doing what they're doing, and I'd tell them why I'm doing what I'm doing here."

Ivone suggested that instead of seeking further contact with the headquarters, "maybe we'll form our own movement here." It would be "autonomous," she added with a twinkle in her eye, referring to the independence the movement has long claimed, but which Ivone was convinced had been lost in recent years. And in the union hall in Sananduva, Rosane told me about meetings where women from different parts of the state discussed getting involved again in the internal politics of the women's movement, to win elections and make the movement more inclusive.

Father Cláudio addressed the issue of difference, in families and political parties, at the 2004 campaign meeting for a coalition of leftist parties in Ibiraiaras. "You sew together the common points to win people over and gain votes," Father Cláudio had counseled, "It's not bad or ugly that there are these differences in families or in the campaign. There's no other *jeito* (no other way to make things work)."

By 2007, however, it was clear that the women who had founded the MMTR now pursued their activism along separate paths rather than holding these together in one overarching movement. As we caught up with the women we knew—women who had together formed the women's movement, against the odds, at a time when their lives were intertwined—we saw how different their paths had become. The women at the movement headquarters had united with rural women's movements in other states to form a national movement, the Movement of Peasant Women, known as the MMC (Movimento de Mulheres Camponesas). The national movement, allied with Via Campesina, emphasizes the struggle for a new agricultural model based on sustainable farming practices and egalitarian local economies. Women's rights, while mentioned among MMC objectives, figure less prominently in their mobilizations, though the movement has begun to focus public attention on domestic violence and continues to provide meeting places for women at demonstrations, in the pharmacies, and in workshops run jointly with other social movements. The office in Passo Fundo functions not only as the headquarters of the state women's movement but also as the national office for the MMC. The women who would not gamble on the institutions of government— including Adriana and Salete, Mari and Carminha, and Izanete—run a national women's movement, linked to the largest national and international movements of rural people in the world, fighting for radical change in the countryside.

For Vera, in contrast, women's issues have become part of a new vision for local government. Vera has been developing this vision of government together with her husband, Celso Prando, since 1997, when she left the MMTR to focus on the farmers' union in Sananduva and eventually become its first woman president. From 1998 to 2002, Celso headed a left-of-center coalition government in Sananduva, a position he won after serving a term as deputy mayor in the preceding administration. Then, as mayor, along with his team from the Workers' Party, he began to articulate and put into practice policies on health, education, and rural economic development to bring economic growth and greater equality to the struggling town. But the leftist coalition had been voted out of office, and Vera wants to develop a progressive vision of her own that could again win elections and govern. In the meantime, Celso is farming their land, trying to establish an enduring economic base for their family after years of paid and unpaid work in movements, the farmers' union, and local government and grappling with what it means to live and work at home while his wife travels around the state.

Like Izanete and Fernando, Gessi and Didi, Rosane and her husband, Vicente —indeed like many of the younger couples we had gotten to know—Vera and

Celso have been forging new ways of balancing home and work in a marriage. There is nothing easy about this, and as Vera indicated to me in our conversations over the years, she does not know precisely what equality means or where the possibility of reshaping gender roles will lead. In this, she and other women in the women's movement are in much the same position as couples in the United States who have tried to make more egalitarian households in recent decades. Many of us now realize that who washes the dishes or picks up the baby or earns the money is only one small piece of the answer. As a close friend put it, "We made many, many, changes in these areas, and that did change some things, but so much inside of us has not changed."[4] Vera knows that who does the dishes is neither the central issue in gaining rights and voice for women nor irrelevant to that effort, and it is surprisingly difficult to change.

As a professor, Elenice researches issues directly related to women, believing that women's movement activists should focus fully on such issues rather than directing their energies to the struggle for a new agricultural development model, which other movements can pursue. When we last spoke with her, Elenice was designing a research project on the incidence of domestic violence in rural households, a phenomenon that everyone agreed was widespread but about which there was no data and little action.

The women's pharmacies bring together women who have otherwise taken different directions, but seek counsel and remedies in the pharmacies. At the pharmacy workshops, members of the national women's movement mingle with women who have rejected the headquarters' militancy and centralization, identifying locally with the MMTR and its banner and refusing to adopt the new national name, with its unfamiliar use of the word *camponesa* (peasant). Leaders who stayed local and joined the government or the unions in their towns, such as Gessi and Vera, also support the pharmacies, recognizing their role in addressing day-to-day needs and connecting those needs to strategies for change in gender roles and local economies. And when the collective of women who ran the pharmacy in Ibiraiaras took over the local organic farmers' market, the Quitanda, they refashioned the store into an outlet for produce, crafts, baked goods, and herbal remedies that also functioned as a gathering place, looking right out over Ibiraiaras's central plaza, for rural women and town dwellers alike.

Activists in the women's movement also pursue activities farther afield from the movement's original goals. One night during our return visit with our curriculum, Marilda Sauthier invited us to dinner at her house, along with several couples we knew, and we headed over there with Gessi and Didi. We had seen Marilda grow in poise and stature in movement activities over the years, and we wondered how her deepening public role at meetings and in the pharmacy affected her home life. After driving for several kilometers on winding, unlit dirt roads, Didi pulled up to the modest, three-room house, con structed through a government housing initiative for rural families, where we had twice before conducted interviews with Marilda and her extended family. We were greeted by the mixture of hesitation and warmth with which many rural families received us and each other. Marilda's formal welcome, however, caught us off guard. "We're happy to offer you *um novo coquetel* (a new cocktail)," she said brightly from the corner of her tiny living room, alongside the TV. Then she introduced the assembled guests to Herbalife, and we watched a DVD, produced in Los Angeles, about the globally marketed nutrition supplement. The DVD was accompanied by tall glasses of Herbalife shakes, along with a smooth sales talk replete with charts and photographs, delivered by Marilda's sister and brother-in-law, Marta and Altamir da Silva, who had long worked as activists for a progressive Catholic Church–based NGO in the region and for leftist municipal governments.

Now Marta and Altamir sold Herbalife in what seemed a classic combination of Mary Kay and pyramid scheme. A healthy modern life, they urged their friends, could be achieved by substituting the Herbalife liquid drink for breakfast and dinner. They emphasized that chubby children like their daughter—as well as overweight adults, as Altamir had been—would become thin and self-confident with the nutrition supplement, while busy working moms saved time in the kitchen. They urged Didi, adrift since his father's death and uncertain about how he and Gessi would support their family, to buy an Herbalife kit and begin selling its products while there was still a wide-open market in their town.

In the car afterward, I realized how shaken Emma was by the presentation, as she confronted having traveled so far—to a place where organic food grew plentifully and mealtimes brought families together—and still encountering slick, prepackaged advertisements for beauty in a bottle and the fastest food imaginable. It scared me too for its ferocious embodiment of the self-help approaches we had seen in some of the pharmacies and for its signaling of yet another direction in which women's movement activists may turn.

The enchantment of the rural women's movement lies in the belief that ordinary people can reform the world at the grassroots, through social-movement organizing and participation in government, so that they can better *ser gente* (be fully human). What the women in the women's movement and many of its offshoots are gambling on is an extension of the post–World War II imaginary of development: the idea that in the modern world, economic growth can bring about decent standards of living and democratic politics can bring about fairness. It's a secular and gradualist vision, even as it is often stimulated by religious commitment and radical leftist politics. And it has expanded beyond the mid-twentieth-century's focus on industrialization and national government to raise issues of racial and gender equality, environmental sustainability, and active local democracy.[5] This vision—of sustaining grassroots politics in a democratic context—is what brings the women in Ibiraiaras and Sananduva to the women's movement meetings and from there to demonstrations in the streets, jobs as union presidents or heads of health departments, and discussions with their own families about who they are and who does the dishes. The enchantment of activism—and the future it envisions and makes tangible in the present—is also what democracy needs to survive in the world today.

In the twentieth and twenty-first centuries, few democracies outside Western Europe have ensured that economic growth meets the basic material needs of nearly all citizens. Few democracies offer dependable commitments to equality before the law and freedom from violence, and none have eliminated deep inequalities of gender, sexuality, and race. But for democracy to be meaningful and valued across the globe, it has to make things better in precisely these ways. And that's what progressive social movements press democracies to do. They rally people behind visions of an alternative future, one where women can speak freely and share fully in decision making or where sustainable small-scale agriculture keeps poor people on the land. In democracies, political parties and elections can prevent the worst abuses of power or throw the scoundrels out, but politicians and public officials rarely think outside the box and innovate so that people can be *mais gente ainda* (more fully human), so that they can eat, go to school, and influence decisions that affect them. Democracies need movements to keep them moving.

But what does it mean to be a movement in democracy? It means to develop all the capacities of selfhood, speech, and mobilization that the MMTR forged over two decades and then go one step further, holding together that multiplicity in one movement, even if it doesn't seem to fit together. Or, if different groups spin off from the original organization, then movement in democracy means keeping them in active dialogue one with the other, openly and without hierarchy, forging complementary strategies.[6]

It turns out that democracy, in a country or a movement, has something in common with father daughter collaboration. In each case, you need both unruly emotions and formal procedures to hold things together and move them forward. Vera regrets not fighting back, not staying in the MMTR, with its rough and tumble, even harsh and mean-spirited, politics. She didn't know how to do this at the time or even think of doing it. The activism she learned from the Catholic Church meant consensus—reaching agreement through discussion—not fighting hard and outmaneuvering your opponents while adhering to agreed-upon democratic procedures.

Recounting one of the earliest demonstrations that the social movements mounted, when young people blocked a major highway and soldiers stood poised to attack them, Gessi remembers how just in the nick of time a bus pulled up carrying Bishop Orlando, short and rotund and fiercely committed to a fair society for all on this earth. The bishop bounded from the bus, passing right through the line of soldiers and preventing them from turning their weapons on the protesters. The priests taught the young people how to speak, how to stand up to the soldiers, and how to use religious symbols and bodies to ward off attack. But there was no tradition or training in the Church for the battles of democratic procedure. And there was no tradition in the old Left and the social movements it most directly shaped, such as the MST, for democratic pluralism. Leftist parties and movements of the first three-quarters of the twentieth century had plenty of experience with grassroots organizing and protest, political battles within existing systems, and revolutionary struggles. But in many instances of radical politics, those arguing for democratic procedures lost out to supporters of centralization and vanguardism who believed it was the task of leaders to determine the right strategy for fostering change and mobilize people to follow it.

But when Gessi went to work in the health department, she was attempting something different and crucial. As a deeply committed activist, she wanted to take on power and reshape it from the inside. She also wanted to work in the institutions and the streets simultaneously. "Wouldn't you rather," I'd asked Salete and Adriana at the MMTR headquarters during our first visit there, "have people who thought like you, with your commitments, inside the institutions, so that you could pressure them from the outside, and that pressure would bear fruit, there would be someone in the institution to listen and follow through?" While the women in the headquarters rejected this stance as too much of a gamble, women in the pharmacies, like Gessi in city hall, were working step-by-step to build something new on the ground.

"Dialogue," Elsi observed at the pharmacy workshop in Santa Lucia, "is when people make exchanges; I say what I think and you say what you think."

"That can be a negative thing if we disagree," Inez countered.

Among rural women in Rio Grande do Sul—the women who ask their husbands for permission to leave the house and the women who defied their fathers to leave and form a movement—there is no cultural or political tradition of argumentative dialogue. For many women, as for Ivone and Vania, balancing silence and speech is perilous. It is that most dangerous ground, where the private becomes public, where pains and fears, shames and uncertainties and daring new acts make you vulnerable in the very moment when you might break free to re-form the world. "As soon as you open up speech," Ivone had observed one night in her kitchen, reflecting on her inability to speak publicly about her relationship with Vania, "you also close it down."

Very few people can do what Gessi does, make her uncertainties part of her successful diplomacy and keep speaking for a future she doesn't know for sure how to reach. For most of the women in the women's movement, it is better some of the time to live with distress and not risk the consequences of the most perilous speech. After all, they have already carved out a new public culture at home, at meetings, and in the law.

After talking to Ivone about the painstaking work of going door to door to speak with women about the goals of the women's movement, and about the obstructions posed to activism by religious belief, I asked her if fighting for reform becomes harder when you are aware of the complexity of people's lives and their ambivalence toward change. Ivone—who served as my guide on winding dirt roads the first time I visited women in their homes, and who says what she thinks without apologies—answered directly, and in an uncharacteristically personal fashion. "Each person is different, each conversation." In order to transform the world, Ivone said, you have to reach inside yourself "for the calm that you most need, that you can only find if you don't try to fit everything together."

The paradox of silence amid speech can be a fearsome burden. It carries the risk, as Ivone knew, that as soon as you speak you must deal with people's responses, and as Vania knew, that when you speak at such a moment, it does not change the world, but leaves you with the responsibility to carry the speech forward. This paradox is also, as Emma and I came to understand, the place where political democracy, like dialogue in a family, is forged.

ACKNOWLEDGMENTS

Jeff

Emma and I have many people to thank, not only for key moments of support, encouragement, and guidance but also for the ongoing conversations that deepened our commitment and brought us to new insights. We are first and foremost indebted to the individuals and families in Ibiraiaras and Sananduva who welcomed us into their homes and meeting halls, responded to our many questions, and shared in our excitement about writing a curriculum and book about the MMTR. We interviewed many more people than are named in these pages, and we are grateful for their patience and tenacity in sharing with us their reflections on the women's movement and twenty-five years of dramatic social change. Gessi Bonês, Ivone Bonês, Ari Benedetti, Vania Zambone, Izanete Colla, Rosane Dalsoglio, Vera Fracasso, Mônica Marchesini, Elenice Pastore, Neuza Pistore, Marilda Sauthier, Odete Toazza, and those in the women's pharmacy in Ibiraiaras turned repeatedly to examine the past and its meaning in the present. Their openness to my daughter and me sustained this project from the beginning.

Olga Falcetto and Ovidio Waldemar opened their house and hearts to us in Porto Alegre, offering friendship and family life on each of our research trips. We thank Arnildo Perinotto and Rosa Salvallágio Perinotto for making their wonderful hotel in Ibiraiaras into a multipurpose home and office, Neuza Pistore and Dirceu Caumo and their neighbors for their generous hospitality in Sananduva, and Roselí and Beto Becker, Clarissa Becker, Claudia Fonseca, Salete Brum da Silveira and Sandra Bacaltchuk for guiding us and making us feel always welcome in Porto Alegre.

Karen Sanchez-Eppler followed this project from the beginning, bringing her wisdom and skill to each draft that Emma and I wrote. Vivienne Bennett, Lacy Crawford, Jill Irvine, Mary Ellen Miller, Pam Petro, Mary Roldán, Mary Jo Salter, Leslie Salzinger, Fred Strebeigh, and Jack Womack read drafts at different stages in our writing, and their keen insights shaped the structure and direction of the book.

Evelina Dagnino invited me to the Program on Culture and Politics at the Universidade Estadual de Campinas (UNICAMP) on a Rockefeller Fellowship and insisted that I visit her hometown of Porto Alegre, thus opening the way to all the research that followed. Zander Navarro told me about the innovative organizing of the Movement of Rural Women Workers and suggested, long before Emma and I ever did our first interviews, that I write a book about the MMTR based on profiles of the women who founded it. Alie van der Schaaf generously shared her own excellent work on the women's movement at the beginning of my research. Cecilia Rodrigues provided expert language instruction. Laura Roush helped us throughout this project by artfully suggesting relevant theorists and reflecting on our insights, so that we could take them further.

The first product of Emma and my joint research was our curriculum "Music, Land, and Women's Rights: Citizens Making Change in Brazil and the U.S." Tina Yalen, who as my ninth-grade social studies teacher showed me how to learn and teach about the world in unconventional ways, helped us make our materials accessible and useful to teachers. Catherine Harris arranged our first workshop with some of her fellow Teach for America teachers in Miami. The directors and outreach coordinators of the Latin America centers at Harvard, Duke, Yale, Brown, and the University of California, San Diego, sponsored workshops on our curriculum for high school teachers, graduate students, and professors. We thank Merilee Grindle, Maria Regan, Jolie Olcott, Tamera Marko, Julia de la Torre, Gil Joseph, Jean Silk, Elena Serapiglia, Christine Hunefeldt, and Jim Green for arranging workshops; Lara Ramsey and Tom Weiner for inviting us into their classrooms at the Smith College Campus School; and Gretchen Laui for arranging to have our workshop at the University of California, San Diego, filmed and brainstorming ways of disseminating the curriculum further.

Starting with my first trip to Brazil in 1996, colleagues there welcomed me and supported my research on social movements. My deepest thanks go to Sergio Baierle, Anita Brumer, Evelina Dagnino, Claudia Fonseca, Olivia Gomez da Cunha, Claudia de Lima Costa, Zander Navarro, and Sergio Schneider for office space, meals, conversation, and responsiveness to all my questions.

Numerous foundations and research institutes have offered generous support for my research in Brazil and writing in the United States: the Rockefeller Foundation, through UNICAMP; the Institute for Advanced Study at Princeton; the Center for the Critical Analysis of Contemporary Culture at Rutgers; the MacArthur Foundation, through the Research and Writing Grant that brought me and my family to Brazil for a year; the Fulbright Foundation; and the American Philosophical Society, through a summer research grant and a sabbatical fellowship.

Valerie Millholland at Duke University Press embraced this book from the first moment we contacted her, and her support and enthusiasm were invaluable as we proceeded from early draft to finished manuscript. Miriam Angress has managed the editorial process with clarity and care, and we thank her for her skillful attention to our work.

Many academic colleagues in the United States have supported me in this unconventional endeavor. Thanks to Peter Berger for making a place for me at the

Institute on Culture, Religion, and World Affairs at Boston University and to Susan Eckstein for encouraging the research I did with Emma. To my colleagues in the CivSoc project (The Inter-University Consortium on Social Movements in the Americas), Sonia Alvarez, Millie Thayer, Gianpaolo Baiocchi, and Agustín Lao-Montes, thank you for the joys and rigors of a five-person collaborative writing project. My deep gratitude, as always, to John Womack Jr., Gil Joseph, Leslie Salzinger, Marc Edelman, Mary Roldán, Ben Junge, Miriam Pawel, and Jeremy Glazer for ongoing conversation and advice on the scholarly and personal issues that matter to me. By offering me a house in New Hampshire in which to work, Millie Thayer and Helen Chapell made writing this book possible. Vivienne Bennett, my collaborator on the Enduring Reform Project, has offered insight and guidance with unstinting generosity.

Thanks to my parents, Bernice and Sheldon Rubin, for their ever-present love and support, including funding for Emma's trip to Ibiraiaras when she was fifteen, and for their ongoing delight in their granddaughters. My mother-in-law, Miriam Sokoloff, hosted writing retreats for Emma and me, and her wit and warmth animated our writing and our family. My daughters Hannah and Esther embraced our family year in Brazil with enthusiasm and accepted this project in their lives and around our dinner table, where they continually forge their own robust and ever-changing model of speech and dialogue, from which all of us learn.

Finally, and most of all, I thank Shoshana Sokoloff for her love, her insights into parenting, her own demanding work and the grace and talent with which she does it, and her willingness to run the household while Emma and I traveled to Brazil and to classrooms near and far. Shoshana has enabled, indeed created, the mix of autonomy and interdependence that makes spaces for speech at home and for action in the wider world. The practice of dialogue and the intimacy of protest are what we learn together.

Emma

I grew up with this project, so it has been shaped by the teachers, mentors, friends, and family who raised me. I wouldn't have had the skills or courage to start this project if it weren't for the amazing teachers I had before it began, including Lara Ramsey, Jan Szymaszek, Elizabeth Cooney, Catherine Gallagher, Gary Huggett, Andy Hilnbrand, Tricia Lea, Bob Brick, and Andrea and Mitch Chakour. Mary Ellen Miller taught me lessons in clarinet and in life every Wednesday from when I was eight to eighteen. Laura Davis and Danika Tyminski let me teach their students while I was still a student myself. My friends at the Pioneer Valley Performing Arts Charter School, Elias, Tiama, Elena, Ian, Meg, Amira, Leah, David, and Molly, supported this project without letting it define me.

I hope I can bring to the people I work with in the future the care, insight, and generosity my professors at Yale showed me. George Chauncey, Richard Deming, Margaret Spillane, and Glenda Gilmore taught me to delve into uncertainties and focus my research on the themes and events that don't fall perfectly into place. Robert Thompson, Lillian Guerra, Cynthia Zarin, Linda Greenhouse, and Reva Siegel pushed my work in new directions. Anne Fadiman taught me to write about topics I once considered outside of my range, and she built a community of writers and friends to which I still turn when struggling to find just the right word. Gil Joseph's classes and our conversations shaped my senior essay, this book, and the way I think about the world. Fred Strebeigh read one, two, or often three drafts of each of my chapters. The directions I take, in writing and in life, are still shaped by his eye for structure and commitment to capturing varied voices.

Several fellowships have made this and other projects possible, from before I started college through the year after graduation. To the Barry, Bates, Bildner, Bronfman, Golub, Linck, Liman, Howland, and Richter fellowships, thank you for your investment in my projects and ideas.

Teachers have taken many different forms. Dean John Loge knew to lend me the "cabin," a fourth-floor office in which I could spread my chapter outlines across the walls. Dean Loge and Rabbi Lauren Holtzblatt taught me and many other students to create cabins and communities wherever we go. Pam Brown and David Hall brought me onto their team at Texas RioGrande Legal Aid. Dale Russakoff and Matt Purdy's dedication to writing and to people means so much to me. Elias Sanchez-Eppler and the whole Sanchez-Eppler and Eppler-Epstein families offered me homes away from home filled with honorary cousins, quiet work spaces, and lively games of dominoes.

Thank you Julia Lurie, Jeannette Penniman, Kate Grace, Thomas Meyer, Kelvin Vu, and all of FOOT '11 for being there at every turn, on backpacking trips and on campus, and for filling 15 Edgewood with friends. Mari Oye (all-star roommate and editor), Rachel Wilf, Tina Kraja, and all of Timothy Dwight College for unbeatable spirit and kindness. Katherine Kendrick, Amila Golic, Catherine Osborn, Rae Ellen Biche, and the whole Globalist team for bringing passion and wit to reporting trips and ed-board meetings. CSP '11 for new and lasting friendships, and for pushing me to say what I believe. Amy Larsen and Sam Schoenburg for afternoon runs and continuing conversations, and Ian Cutler and Nora Caplan-Bricker for bringing some of the Pioneer Valley to college. And Sam Purdy, who brings people together wherever he is. I've never stopped feeling lucky for Sam's belief in this project and in me.

When I think of changes, I think of Gessi, Ivone, Vania, Mônica, Vera, Elenice, and all the women in Brazil who let Dad and me into their lives. I hope they sense how much we have learned from them, about the challenge of speech and the costs of silence, and about the power of ordinary people to change their communities and change themselves.

Like Ivone, I also think of my own family. Savta and Grandma and Grandpa taught me the art of asking questions and always found time to answer mine. Hannah and Esther balance silliness with insight, courage with honesty, talent with care. I mean it when I say I look up to my younger sisters. All three of us look up to our mom, whose knowledge, poise, and generosity touches everyone at work and at home. Her ideas and experiences have shaped who I am, and the way I think and write is due in large part to the love and dedication with which Mom approaches the world.

NOTES

Chapter 1: Leaving Home

Unless otherwise noted, the experiences, conversations, and quotations related in this book come from our interviews and participant observation in Ibiraiaras, Sananduva, Passo Fundo, and nearby towns during a series of research trips between 1997 and 2008. In addition to attending political and social events and spending extensive periods of time with individual families, we carried out more than fifty in-depth interviews, between one and three hours each in length, all in Portuguese and some videotaped. We interviewed movement leaders and participants, women who do not participate in the movement, family members of activists in the women's movement, priests, nuns, politicians, union leaders, academics, and staff members of local NGOs. Our understanding of the history of the movement and how it changed over time also draws on secondary sources on the MMTR and the economy of Rio Grande do Sul, as well as more than twenty years of women's movement newsletters and pamphlets.

1. For an outline of the economy of Rio Grande do Sul and how it has changed since the 1970s, see Sergio Schneider and Paulo André Niederle, "Resistance Strategies and Diversification of Rural Livelihoods: The Construction of Autonomy among Brazilian Family Farmers," *The Journal of Peasant Studies* 37, no. 2 (April 2010): 379–405; Zander Navarro, "Democracia, cidadania e representação: Os movimentos sociais rurais no estado do Rio Grande do Sul, Brasil, 1978–1990," in *Política, protesto e cidadania no campo: As lutas sociais dos colonos e dos trabalhadores rurais no Rio Grande do Sul*, edited by Zander Navarro (Porto Alegre: Editora da Universidade/ UFRGS, 1996), 62–105; and Alice van der Schaaf, *Jeito de mulher rural: A busca de direitos sociais e da igualdade de gênero no Rio Grande do Sul* (Passo Fundo: Editora Universidade de Passo Fundo, 2001), 82–97.

2. For a basic introduction to the history of the Catholic Church and the emergence of liberation theology in Brazil, see Thomas C. Bruneau, *The Church in Brazil: The Politics of Religion* (Austin: University of Texas Press, 1982); and Scott Mainwaring, *The Catholic Church and Politics in Brazil, 1916–1985* (Stanford: Stanford University Press, 1986). For the impact of the Church on social-movement activism, see Ana Maria Doimo, *A vez e a voz do popular: Movimentos sociais e participação política no Brasil pós-70* (Rio de Janeiro: Relume Dumará, 1995).

3. On the politics of the military regime and its use of torture, see Thomas E. Skidmore, *The Politics of Military Rule in Brazil, 1964–1985* (Oxford: Oxford University Press, 1990); Maria Helena Moreira Alves, *State and Opposition in Military Brazil* (Austin: University of Texas Press, 1988); and A. J. Langguth, *Hidden Terrors: The Truth About U.S. Police Operations in Latin America* (New York: Pantheon, 1979).

Chapter 2: Transforming Southern Brazil

1. For a guide to politics and social life in nineteenth-century Brazil, see Emilia Viotti da Costa, *The Brazilian Empire: Myths and Histories* (Chapel Hill: University of North Carolina Press, 2000). On the aftermath of slavery, see George Reid Andrews, *Blacks and Whites in São Paulo, 1888–1988* (Madison: University of Wisconsin Press, 1991).

2. On official and elite recognition of Afro-Brazilian culture as part of Brazil's national culture, see Hermano Vianna, *The Mystery of Samba: Popular Music and National Identity in Brazil* (Chapel Hill: University of North Carolina Press, 1999). On the inclusion of urban workers into a national labor and social welfare system, see Kenneth Paul Erickson, *The Brazilian Corporative State and Working-Class Politics* (Berkeley: University of California Press, 1977); and Barbara Weinstein, *For Social Peace in Brazil: Industrialists and the Remaking of the Working Class in São Paulo, 1920–1964* (Chapel Hill: University of North Carolina Press, 1996).

3. In her diary, published as *Child of the Dark*, Carolina Maria de Jesus paints a vivid picture of daily life, hunger, and deprivation in a *favela* (shantytown) in São Paulo in the 1950s (New York: Dutton, 1962). For an equally vivid portrayal of hunger and poverty in northeast Brazil, see Nancy Scheper-Hughes, *Death without Weeping: The Violence of Everyday Life in Brazil* (Berkeley: University of California Press, 1993). On crime, drugs, and violence in Rio's favelas in the 2000s, see Robert Gay, *Lucia: Testimonies of a Brazilian Drug Dealer's Woman* (Philadelphia: Temple University Press, 2005); and Enrique Desmond Arias, *Drugs and Democracy in Rio de Janeiro: Trafficking, Social Networks, and Public Security* (Chapel Hill: University of North Carolina Press, 2006). In *Favela: Four Decades of Living on the Edge in Rio de Janeiro* (New York: Oxford University Press, 2010), Janice Perlman provides a forty-year perspective on the social conditions of favelas and their role in the Brazilian and global economies.

4. On the changing rural economy of Rio Grande do Sul, see note 1 in Chapter 1. Also see G. A. Banck, "The Insertion of Household Farms into Modern Brazilian Agrarian Structure: The Case of the Ijuí Region, Rio Grande do Sul," in *Sowing the Whirlwind: Soya Expansion and Social Change in Southern Brazil*, edited by G. A. Banck and K. den Boer (Amsterdam: CEDLA, 1991), chapter 4. On the establishment of rural unions under the military government and the emergence of more radical and democratic unions, see Zander Navarro, "Democracia, cidadania e representação: Os movimentos sociais rurais no estado do Rio Grande do Sul, Brasil, 1978–1990," in *Política, protesto e cidadania no campo: As lutas sociais dos colonos e dos trabalhadores rurais no Rio Grande do Sul*, edited by Zander Navarro (Porto Alegre: Editora da Universidade/UFRGS, 1996), 62–105; Peter P. Houtzager, "State and Unions in the Transformation of the Brazilian Countryside, 1964–1979," *Latin American Research Review* 33, no. 2 (1998): 103–42; Everton Lazaretti Picolotto, *Mundo Agrario*, 9, no. 18, 2009, http://www.mundoagrario; Biorn Maybury-Lewis, *The Politics of the Possible: The Brazilian Rural Workers' Trade Union Movement, 1964–1985* (Philadelphia: Tem-

ple University Press, 1994); and Claudia Job Schmitt, "A CUT dos colonos: Histórias da construção de um novo sindicalismo no campo no Rio Grande do Sul," in Navarro, *Política, protesto e cidadania no campo*, 189–226. On the position of women in rural areas of Brazil's south and northeast, women's growing role in the unions and women's movements, and the resistance of rural unions and of the MST to women's claims, see Carmen Diana Deere, "Women's Land Rights and Rural Social Movements in the Brazilian Agrarian Reform," *Journal of Agrarian Change*, 3, nos. 1 and 2 (January and April 2003): 257–88.

5. Sergio Schneider and Paulo André Niederle, "Resistance Strategies and Diversification of Rural Livelihoods: The Construction of Autonomy among Brazilian Family Farmers," *The Journal of Peasant Studies* 37, no. 2 (April 2010): 384. These percentages are averages across Brazil's three southernmost states, Rio Grande do Sul, Santa Catarina, and Paraná.

6. A panorama of the rural social movements of the 1980s in Rio Grande do Sul, with concise histories of each of them, appears in Navarro, *Política, protesto e cidadania no campo*. For a presentation and analysis of key urban social movements of the period, see Ana Maria Doimo, *A vez e a voz do popular: Movimentos sociais e participação política no Brasil pós-70* (Rio de Janeiro: Relume Dumará, 1995).

7. In understanding the many layers of culture and power that women face when they fight to gain rights and change gender roles, we have been schooled by feminist scholarship generally, as well as by the growing body of work on gender in Latin America that has examined economics, culture, and politics in the nineteenth and twentieth centuries. We have been particularly influenced by the work of Christine Hunefelt on domestic violence and legal rights (*Liberalism in the Bedroom: Quarreling Spouses in Nineteenth-Century Lima* [University Park: Pennsylvania State University Press, 2000]); Donna Guy on women's work and public health (*Sex and Danger in Buenos Aires: Prostitution, Family, and Nation in Argentina* [Lincoln: University of Nebraska Press, 1991]); Nancy Scheper-Hughes on how women's intimate relationships are shaped by poverty and violence (*Death without Weeping*); Leslie Salzinger on gender roles, bodies, and labor control (*Genders in Production: Making Workers in Mexico's Global Factories* [Berkeley: University of California Press, 2003]); Lynn Stephen on women's movements in zones of crisis (*Women and Social Movements in Latin America: Power from Below* [Austin: University of Texas Press, 1997]); Donna M. Goldstein on speech and humor in negotiating intimate relationships (*Laughter Out of Place: Race, Class, Violence, and Sexuality in a Rio Shantytown* [Berkeley: University of California Press, 2003]); and the work of Sonia Alvarez on Latin American feminisms ("Advocating Feminism: The Latin American Feminist NGO 'Boom,'" *International Feminist Journal of Politics* 1, no. 2 [November 1999]: 181–209; and, with Elisabeth Jay Friedman, Ericka Beckman, Maylei Blackwell, Norma Stoltz Chinchilla, Nathalie Lebon, Marysa Navarro, and Marcela Ríos Tobar, "Encountering Latin American and Caribbean Feminisms," *Signs: Journal of Women in Culture and Society* 28, no. 2 [2003]: 537–79).

8. The authors in Alfred Stepan, ed., *Democratizing Brazil: Problems of Transition*

and Consolidation (New York: Oxford University Press, 1989) examine the stages, components, and risks of Brazil's transition to democracy. In *The Workers' Party and Democratization in Brazil* (New Haven: Yale University Press, 1995), Margaret Keck examines the origins of the Workers' Party. Sonia Alvarez discusses the growth of urban women's movements in Brazil during the dictatorship and transition to democracy in *Engendering Democracy in Brazil: Women's Movements in Transition Politics* (Princeton: Princeton University Press, 1990).

9. Alice van der Schaaf (*Jeito de mulher rural: A busca de direitos sociais e da igualdade de gênero no Rio Grande do Sul* [Passo Fundo: Editora Universidade de Passo Fundo, 2001) offers a detailed account of the formation of the MMTR, its social context, and its early activities. My brief account of the MMTR's history draws primarily on van der Schaaf's work, in addition to our interviews. Lynn Stephen provides a briefer analysis in "Class, Gender, and Autonomy: The Rural Women Workers' Movement of Southern Brazil," in *Women and Social Movements in Latin America*, 209–33, as does Anita Brumer in "Mobilization and the Quest for Recognition: The Struggle of Rural Women in Southern Brazil for Access to Welfare Benefits," in *Welfare, Poverty, and Development in Latin America*, edited by C. Abel and C. M. Lewis (Basingstoke, UK: Macmillan Press, 1993), 405–20. For discussions of Brazilian rural women's movements more generally, especially in the south, see also Deere, "Women's Land Rights and Rural Social Movements in the Brazilian Agrarian Reform"; and Julia S. Guivant, "Agrarian Change, Gender, and Land Rights: A Brazilian Case Study," United Nations Research Institute for Social Development, Social Policy and Development Programme, paper no. 14, June 2003. Millie Thayer's *Making Transnational Feminism: Rural Women, NGO Activists, and Northern Donors in Brazil* (New York: Routledge, 2010) provides excellent comparative material on the rural women's movement in the northeastern state of Pernambuco. For a recent collection on the rights and roles of women in rural Brazil, see *Gênero e geração em contextos rurais*, edited by Parry Scott, Rosineide Cordeiro, and Marilda Menezes (Florianópolis: Editora Mulheres, 2010).

10. The MMTR in Rio Grande do Sul consistently worked to theorize class and gender together and to promote policies in both areas, though the nature of their theorizing and the way they balanced these issues in practice changed over time, with class coming to the fore in the statewide movement in the 2000s (MMTR newsletters, 1991–2004, and Paludo, Conceição and Venderléia L. P. Daron, *Gênero, Classe e Projeto Popular: Compreender mais para lutar melhor*. Passo Pundo: Gráfica Batistel, 2001.) Race, in contrast, was neither theorized nor addressed directly by the movement, which consisted predominantly of light-skinned women of European descent, reflect the demographics of rural Rio Grande do Sul. While attention to beliefs about race and the way racial divides may have been enacted would undoubtedly have nuanced our analysis of internal tensions and exclusions within the MMTR, in getting at just those kinds of issues—of exclusions, of silences, of difficulties of dialogue and democracy—we found it most productive to address the ones raised and enacted most visibly by the women themselves. Thus we focused on exclusions based on

differing political positions, on internal decision-making procedures, on the difficulties and shame of speaking of pain and violence, on where and how to do politics, and on sexuality. Deeper exploration of race, which would have meant going beyond the issues women themselves raised out of their daily experiences, would have complemented and extended this analysis.

11. Van der Schaaf, *Jeito de mulher rural*, 154–57; Stephen, *Women and Social Movements in Latin America*, 219. Accurate data on statewide MMTR membership is difficult to obtain, and these numbers are approximate.

12. Van der Schaaf, *Jeito de mulher rural*, 174; Deere, "Women's Land Rights and Rural Social Movements in the Brazilian Agrarian Reform," 276.

13. Schneider and Niederle, "Resistance Strategies," 391–99.

14. Our thinking about the work that movements do, including the kinds of publics they produce and the way they weave visions of the future into the present, has been shaped by Michael Warner, *Publics and Counterpublics* (New York: Zone Books, 2005); and Reinhart Koselleck, *Futures Past: On the Semantics of Historical Time* (New York: Columbia University Press, 2004).

15. Van der Schaaf, *Jeito de mulher rural*, analyzes the roles of feminist advisors to the MMTR, the resistances they encountered, and the ways they modified their interventions as a result (234–37).

Chapter 3: Family Ties

1. For accounts of these movements, see Gianpaolo Baiocchi, *Militants and Citizens: The Politics of Participatory Democracy in Porto Alegre* (Stanford: Stanford University Press, 2005); Wendy Wolford, *This Land Is Ours Now: Social Mobilization and the Meaning of Land in Brazil* (Durham, NC: Duke University Press, 2010); and Patrick Neate and Damian Platt, *Culture Is Our Weapon: Making Music and Changing Lives* (New York: Penguin, 2010).

2. My analysis of the formation of the Zapotec movement COCEI and its radical opposition to the Mexican government over the course of two decades can be found in Jeffrey W. Rubin, *Decentering the Regime: Ethnicity, Radicalism, and Democracy in Juchitán, Mexico* (Durham, NC: Duke University Press, 1997).

3. On Zapotec medical practices and the cultural roles of Isthmus Zapotec midwives, see Shoshana R. Sokoloff, "The Proud Midwives of Juchitán," in *Histories, Politics, and Representations from Juchitán, Oaxaca*, edited by Howard Campbell, Leigh Binford, Miguel Bartolome, and Alicia Barabas (Washington, DC: Smithsonian Institution Press, 1993), 267–77.

4. On cultural and religious responses to globalization, see Aihwa Ong, *Neoliberalism as Exception: Mutations in Citizenship and Sovereignty* (Durham, NC: Duke University Press, 2006); Jean Comaroff and John Comaroff, "Millennial Capitalism and the Culture of Neoliberalism," in *Millennial Capitalism and the Culture of Neoliberalism*, edited by John L. Comaroff and Robert P. Weller (Durham, NC: Duke University Press, 2001), 1–56; and Laura Roush, "Notes on the Gift Exchange at Alfarería: Image

and Liturgies of the Culto a la Santa Muerte in Mexico City," paper presented at the Latin American Studies Association, San Juan, Puerto Rico, March 15–18, 2006.

Chapter 4: Gambling on Change

1. The opportunity to work in government during the Lula administration brought both benefits and risks, and there has been ongoing debate about the balance. See Jeffrey W. Rubin, "Can Democracy Take on Empire in Lula's Brazil?," in *Empire and Dissent: The United States and Latin America*, edited by Fred Rosen (Durham, NC: Duke University Press, 2008), 162–87; Hilary Wainwright and Sue Branford, *In the Eye of the Storm: Left-Wing Activists Discuss the Political Crisis in Brazil* (Amsterdam: Trans National Institute, 2006); and Wendy Hunter and Timothy J. Power, "Lula's Brazil at Midterm," *Journal of Democracy* 16, no. 3 (July 2005): 127–39.

2. Many local activists in Rio Grande do Sul disliked the name change, continuing to think of themselves as "rural workers" rather than "peasants" and rejecting the idea of one single term to be applied to rural people across Brazil and internationally. For this reason, we continue to use the term MMTR to describe the local organizations in Ibiraiaras and Sananduva, even after the formation of the national movement in 2003.

Chapter 5: Fighting for Rights in Latin America

1. David Bushnell and Neill Macaulay recount the postindependence construction of Latin American nations as a series of elite contests and accommodations (*The Emergence of Latin America in the Nineteenth Century* [Oxford: Oxford University Press, 1994]). Florencia Mallon highlights the repeated mobilizations, pressures, and visions that peasants in Peru and Mexico brought to this process (*Peasant and Nation: The Making of Postcolonial Mexico and Peru* [Berkeley: University of California Press, 1995]).

2. John Womack Jr. offers a detailed account of the tensions within the old order and the path of the revolution that overthrew it (*Zapata and the Mexican Revolution* [New York: Vintage Books, 1970]). Nora Hamilton shows the economic and political underpinnings of the mixed legacy of Lázaro Cárdenas (*The Limits of State Autonomy: Post-Revolutionary Mexico* [Princeton: Princeton University Press, 1982]). Gil Joseph and Daniel Nugent's edited collection, *Everyday Forms of State Formation: Revolution and the Negotiation of Rule in Modern Mexico*, underscores the multiple ways in which the Cárdenas project was enacted and sustained through cultural means (Durham, NC: Duke University Press, 1994).

3. Hermano Vianna, *The Mystery of Samba: Popular Music and National Identity in Brazil* (Chapel Hill: University of North Carolina Press, 1999); George Reid Andrews, *Blacks and Whites in São Paulo, 1888–1988* (Madison: University of Wisconsin Press, 1991); and Barbara Weinstein, *For Social Peace in Brazil: Industrialists and the Remaking of the Working Class in São Paulo, 1920–1964* (Chapel Hill: University of North Carolina Press, 1996).

4. Daniel James, *Resistance and Integration: Peronism and the Argentine Working Class, 1946–1976* (Cambridge: Cambridge University Press, 1994), 33. James offers a nuanced evaluation of Peronism.

5. Carolina Maria de Jesus, *Child of the Dark* (New York: Dutton, 1962), 17.

6. On the Yarur Mill and the political context of the Allende government, see Peter Winn, *Weavers of Revolution: The Yarur Workers and Chile's Road to Socialism* (Oxford: Oxford University Press, 1986).

7. Ibid., 180.

8. The period of military coups, dictatorship, and torture in Latin America from the 1960s to the 1980s has been written about in a wide variety of forms. For references concerning Brazil, see chapter 1, note 3. For a precursor to the later coups, see Stephen Schlesinger, Stephen Kinzer, and John H. Coatsworth, *Bitter Fruit: The Story of the American Coup in Guatemala, Revised and Expanded* (Cambridge, MA: David Rockefeller Center for Latin American Studies, 2005), which discusses the CIA-sponsored coup against the leftist Jacobo Arbenz in Guatemala in 1954. On military brutality, see Beatriz Manz, *Refugees of a Hidden War: The Aftermath of the Counterinsurgency in Guatemala* (Albany: State University of New York Press, 1988); and Jennifer Schirmer, *The Guatemalan Military Project: A Violence Called Democracy* (Philadelphia: University of Pennsylvania Press, 1999). For a seminal account of imprisonment and torture in Argentina, see Jacobo Timerman's memoir *Prisoner without a Name, Cell without a Number* (Madison: University of Wisconsin Press, 2002). For documentation of the role of the United States, see Peter Kornbluh, *The Pinochet File: A Declassified Dossier on Atrocity and Accountability* (New York: New Press, 2003). Films on the military dictatorship include Patricio Guzman's *The Battle of Chile* (1975, 1976, 1978) and *Chile, Obstinate Memory* (1998); on Argentina, see Luis Puenzo's *The Official Story* (1985); and on Brazil, see Burno Barreto's *Four Days in September* (1997). In their four-volume study, *The Breakdown of Democratic Regimes* (Baltimore: The Johns Hopkins University Press, 1978), Juan Linz and Alfred Stepan and their contributors assess the political causes of the coups and subsequent military governments. On the construction of memory and the way that memories of dictatorship continue to shape political positions and choices in the present, see Steve J. Stern's trilogy, *Remembering Pinochet*, *Battling for Hearts and Minds*, and *Reckoning with Pinochet* (Durham, NC: Duke University Press, 2006, 2006, 2010).

9. Winn, *Weavers of Revolution*, 249.

10. Ibid., 252.

11. For a political science perspective on these transitions, written soon after they began, see the four-volume set edited by Guillermo O'Donnell, Philippe Schmitter, and Lawrence Whitehead, *Transitions from Authoritarian Rule* (Baltimore: The Johns Hopkins University Press, 1986), and especially the final synthetic volume, coauthored by O'Donnell and Schmitter, *Tentative Conclusions about Uncertain Democracies*.

12. On social movements in Latin America in the 1980s and 1990s, see Arturo Escobar and Sonia Alvarez, eds., *The Making of Social Movements: Identity, Strategy, and Democracy* (Boulder: Westview Press, 1992); and Sonia Alvarez, Evelina Dagnino,

and Arturo Escobar, eds., *Culture of Politics/Politics of Culture: Re-visioning Latin American Social Movements* (Boulder: Westview Press, 1998).

13. For an early analysis of the effects of globalization, see Barbara Stallings and Wilson Peres, *Growth, Employment, and Equity: The Impact of the Economic Reforms in Latin America and the Caribbean* (Washington, DC: Brookings Institution Press, 2000). For a perspective focusing on international economic institutions, see Joseph E. Stiglitz, *Globalization and Its Discontents* (New York: W. W. Norton, 2003).

14. Enrique Desmond Arias and Daniel M. Goldstein, eds., *Violent Democracies in Latin America* (Durham, NC: Duke University Press, 2010).

Chapter 7: Six Meetings

1. Several authors have influenced our understanding of women's movement meetings and the ways in which they foster activist politics. See Michael Warner, *Publics and Counterpublics* (New York: Zone Books, 2005); and Reinhart Koselleck, *Futures Past: On the Semantics of Historical Time* (New York: Columbia University Press, 2004); David Shulman, *Dark Hope: Working for Peace in Israel and Palestine* (Chicago: University of Chicago Press, 2007); and Walter Benjamin, *Illuminations: Essays and Reflections* (New York: Schocken, 1969). The four consider, respectively, the creation of alternative publics; the interrelationship of future and present; the loneliness and tenacity of protest in the streets; and the role of redemption in visions of the future. Our analysis has also been shaped by work on the role of enchantment and affect in political engagement, including Jane Bennett, *The Enchantment of Modern Life: Attachments, Crossings, and Ethics* (Princeton: Princeton University Press, 2001); Jonathan Flatley, *Affective Mapping: Melancholia and the Politics of Modernism* (Cambridge: Harvard University Press, 2008); David Kyuman Kim, *Melancholic Freedom: Agency and the Spirit of Politics* (Oxford: Oxford University Press, 2007); and Raymond Williams, *Marxism and Literature* (New York: Oxford University Press, 1977).

2. Alice van der Schaaf, *Jeito de mulher rural: A busca de direitos sociais e da igualdade de gênero no Rio Grande do Sul* (Passo Fundo: Editora Universidade de Passo Fundo, 2001), 169, 221–22.

3. On the MST, see chapter 11, note 3.

4. Augusto Boal, *Theater of the Oppressed* (New York: Theater Communications Group, 1993).

Chapter 8: Intimate Protest

1. Reinhart Koselleck, *Futures Past: On the Semantics of Historical Time* (New York: Columbia University Press, 2004), 41.

2. Mariza Scariot e Lúcia M. Görgen, *Mulheres Conquistando Saúde* (Passo Fundo: Gráfica e Editora Pe. Berthier, 1996).

Chapter 9: Demanding Speech and Enduring Silence

1. George Chauncey's work shaped our thinking about Ivone and Vania's story, particularly his concept of "rules of engagement," the unwritten rules people often face in their interactions with colleagues, family, and friends (personal conversation with Chauncey, April 27, 2010). On U.S. gay and lesbian history, see Chauncey's *Gay New York: Gender, Urban Culture, and the Making of the Gay Male World* (New York: Basic Books, 1994); and Martin Bauml Duberman, Martha Vicinus, and George Chauncey, eds., *Hidden from History: Reclaiming the Gay and Lesbian Past* (New York: Dutton, 1989). On silence, see also John Howard's *Men Like That: A Southern Queer History* (Chicago: University of Chicago Press, 1999) and Elizabeth Lapovsky Kennedy, "'But We Would Never Talk about It': The Structures of Lesbian Discretion in South Dakota, 1928–1933," in *Inventing Lesbian Cultures in America*, edited by Ellen Lewin (Boston: Beacon, 1996), 15–39. Ben Junge, assistant professor of anthropology at the State University of New York, New Paltz, provided guidance in incorporating existing scholarship on gay and lesbian history while still "leaving conceptual room for configurations of desire, behavior and identity that don't conform" to frameworks based on U.S. history (e-mail exchange, April 12, 2010).

Chapter 11: Movements in Democracy

1. On the critique within anthropology that gathered momentum in the 1980s and brought key issues of power relations and interpretation into view, see James Clifford and George E. Marcus, eds., *Writing Culture* (Berkeley: University of California Press, 1986). For more recent discussion of the ethics and dynamics of field research pertaining to Latin America, see C. R. Hale, ed., *Engaging Contradictions: Theory, Politics, and Methods of Activist Scholarship* (Berkeley: University of California Press, 2008); and Kay Warren, "Perils and Promises of Engaged Anthropology: Historical Transitions and Ethnographic Dilemmas," in *Engaged Observer: Anthropology, Advocacy, and Activism*, edited by V. Sanford and A. Angel-Ajani (New Brunswick, NJ: Rutgers University Press, 2006), 213–27.

2. This understanding of paradoxes, and the relationship between future and present, draws on a conversation with Laura Roush.

3. While there is general agreement on the radical and anti-institutional political position of the MST (and its modifications in practice), there is considerable controversy concerning the internal practices of the movement and the extent to which it might be considered democratic, in terms of voice, accountability, and dissent. While the MST has favored hierarchy, centralized decision making, male leadership, and the dissemination of prescribed ideological positions, it has also responded over time to internal dissent and new proposals, for example with regard to women's land rights and to sustainable agricultural practices. The MST has succeeded against great odds in giving voice to Brazil's rural poor and putting land reform on the national and international agenda, and it enjoys widespread support on the left in Brazil and internationally.

For a strong critique of the MST, including its internal practices, see Zander Navarro, "The Brazilian Landless Movement (MST): Critical Times," REDES, 15, no. 1 (January/April 2010): 196–223. For analyses that cover the movement's origins, strategies, and successes, see Bernardo Mançano Fernandes, *A formação do MST no Brasil* (Petrópolis, Brazil: Editora Vozes, 2000); John L. Hammond, "Law and Disorder: The Brazilian Landless Farmworkers' Movement," *Bulletin of Latin American Research* 18, no. 4 (1999): 469–89; and Miguel Carter, "The Origins of Brazil's Landless Rural Worker's Movement (MST): The Natalino Episode in Rio Grande do Sul (1981–84), A Case of Ideal Interest Mobilization," Centre for Brazilian Studies Working Paper CBS 43–03, Oxford University, 2003. For the most ethnographically detailed and politically balanced work on the MST, see Wendy Wolford, *This Land Is Ours Now: Social Mobilization and the Meaning of Land in Brazil* (Durham, NC: Duke University Press, 2010). On status differences and disciplinary mechanisms in MST encampments, see Nashieli Rangel Loera, "'Encampment Time': An Anthropological analysis of land occupations in Brazil," *Journal of Peasant Studies* 37, no. 2 (April 2010): 285–318. Carmen Diana Deere ("Women's Land Rights and Rural Social Movements in the Brazilian Agrarian Reform," *Journal of Agrarian Change* 3, nos. 1 and 2 [January and April 2003]: 257–88) and Julia S. Guivant ("Agrarian Change, Gender, and Land Rights: A Brazilian Case Study," United Nations Research Institute for Social Development, Social Policy and Development Programme, paper no. 14, June 2003) focus on rural women's rights, particularly rights to land ownership, and find the MST only minimally responsive to women's claims. On the subordinate position of women in encampments, see Ruti Caldeira, "The Failed Marriage between Women and the Landless People's Movement (MST) in Brazil," *Journal of International Women's Studies* 10, no. 4 (May 2009): 237–58.

Our characterizations of the MST and Via Campesina as hierarchical and resistant to dissent are rooted in the perceptions of the women we interviewed. This characterization of the MST is supported by Wolford's account of the establishment and functioning of MST settlements in southern and northeast Brazil. The literature on Via Campesina suggests that its hierarchical structure in Rio Grande do Sul is not characteristic of the organization in other parts of the world. For background on Via Campesina, see Saturnino M. Borras, "La Vía Campesina and Its Global Campaign for Agrarian Reform," in *Transnational Agrarian Movements Confronting Globalization*, edited by Saturnino M. Borras Jr., Marc Edelman, and Cristóbal Kay (West Sussex, UK: Wiley-Blackwell, 2008), 91–122.

4. I have drawn here on conversations with my friend Karen Sanchez-Eppler, who is Professor of English and of American Studies at Amherst College.

5. Amartya Sen presents a present-day version of this imaginary, focusing on people's capacities to achieve their goals and desires as they understand them. While Sen places more faith in markets than would many Brazilian activists, his focus on capacities avoids the mid-twentieth-century emphasis on industrial growth and Western democratic forms, as well as the underlying anticommunist thrust of much previous development policy (*Development as Freedom* [New York: Alfred A. Knopf, 1999]).

Latin American feminists fighting for new and expanded roles for women, as well as alternative conceptions of gender and sexuality, do so, like Sen, largely within Western conceptions of modernity, while pressing at its boundaries and challenging its exclusions (Sonia Alvarez, Elisabeth Jay Friedman, Ericka Beckman, Maylei Blackwell, Norma Stoltz Chinchilla, Nathalie Lebon, Marysa Navarro, and Marcela Ríos Tobar, "Encountering Latin American and Caribbean Feminisms," *Signs: Journal of Women in Culture and Society* 28, no. 2 [2003]: 537–79).

In contrast, Arturo Escobar rejects the twentieth century's imaginary of development, which he sees as both Western and colonialist, and writes on alternative modernities and movements that seek to achieve them (*Territories of Difference: Place, Movements, Life, Redes* [Durham, NC: Duke University Press, 2008]). Partha Chatterjee, like Escobar, rejects the notion of an inclusive and potentially progressive civil society. In *The Politics of the Governed: Reflections on Popular Politics in Most of the World* (New York: Columbia University Press, 2006), Chatterjee argues that only a privileged set of actors have access to the procedures of democratic politics and bureaucratic institutions.

Discerning more at play and more potential in civil society and citizenship, James Holston argues that poor Brazilians, long excluded from meaningful political participation, take citizenship and political institutions seriously as they fight for rights and well-being in democratic Brazil (*Insurgent Citizenship: Disjunctions of Democracy and Modernity in Brazil* [Princeton: Princeton University Press, 2009]). Evelina Dagnino and her contributors make a similar case in *Sociedade civil e espaços públicos no Brasil* (São Paulo: Paz e Terra, 2002).

6. I thank the students in my 2008 seminar on social movements at Boston University for wrestling with this question as they discussed an earlier draft of this book, and Jeff Stein for pointing the class to the possibility of a different form of splitting apart, one that would involve horizontal communication and alliances rather than antagonism. In 2011, the protest movements that swept the world—from demonstrations in Tahrir Square to the Indignado mobilizations in Spain, the Chilean student movement, and the Occupy Wall Street encampments—each grappled with this issue of how to contain difference within one movement in a democratic manner or, alternately, create alliances of related but separate movements.

INDEX

Page numbers in *italics* refer to photographs.

Jeffrey W. Rubin is an associate professor in the Department of History at Boston University and research associate at Boston University's Institute on Culture, Religion, and World Affairs. He is the author of *Decentering the Regime: Ethnicity, Radicalism, and Democracy in Juchitán, Mexico,* also published by Duke University Press.

Emma Sokoloff-Rubin, a recent Yale graduate, is a Howland Research Fellow in Buenos Aires.

Library of Congress Cataloging-in-Publication Data
Rubin, Jeffrey W.
Sustaining activism : a Brazilian women's movement and a father-daughter collaboration / Jeffrey W. Rubin and Emma Sokoloff-Rubin.
p. cm.
Includes bibliographical references and index.
ISBN 978-0-8223-5406-2 (cloth : alk. paper)
ISBN 978-0-8223-5421-5 (pbk. : alk. paper)
1. Women—Political activity—Brazil.
2. Women in development—Political activity—Brazil.
3. Fathers and daughters—Political activity—Brazil.
I. Sokoloff-Rubin, Emma, 1989– II. Title.
HQ1236.5.B6R83 2013
305.40981—dc23
2012044754